C000201152

Margaret Hockney
My Mother is not
Your Mother

Laura Hockney   *January 1973*
Mother of Margaret – Paul – Philip – John and David

Margaret Hockney
My Mother is not Your Mother

SALTS

SALTS MILL
2017

Text © Margaret Hockney 2017

Published November 2017

Published by
Salts Estates Ltd
Shipley, Saltaire
West Yorkshire
BD18 3LA

ISBN 9780951695081

With Thanks to David Hockney for his kind
permission to reproduce the following work:

Coverpage made from:
'Margaret Hockney 14th,15th,16th August 2015'
from the series of '82 Portraits and 1 Still Life'
Acrylic on Canvas 121.9 x 91.4 cm
© David Hockney

'My Parents' 1977 Oil on Canvas 72" x 72"
© David Hockney

'Margeret and Ken 16th June 2003'
Photographs of 2 watercolour sketches printed
as one image on A4 paper by Margaret Hockney
© David Hockney

Edited by Jim Greenhalf

Designed and prepared for the press by
Derek Brown and Jackie Maidment
derekbrown.design@gmail.com
jackiemaidment.design@gmail.com

Printed in the UK by Gomer Press Ltd
Ceredigion SA44 4JL

Contents

Dedicated to my deceased parents, Laura and Kenneth. Without them there would be no story. I know they meant well, and they were born in such a very different era to mine.

Abou Ben Adhem (may his tribe increase!)
Awoke one night from a deep dream of peace,
And saw, within the moonlight in his room,
Making it rich, and like a lily in bloom,
An angel writing in a book of gold: —
Exceeding peace had made Ben Adhem bold,
And to the presence in the room he said,
"What writest thou?"—The vision raised its head,
And with a look made of all sweet accord,
Answered, "The names of those who love the Lord."
"And is mine one?" said Abou. "Nay, not so,"
Replied the angel. Abou spoke more low,
But cheerly still; and said, "I pray thee, then,
Write me as one that loves his fellow men."
The angel wrote, and vanished. The next night
It came again with a great wakening light,
And showed the names whom love of God had blest,
And lo! Ben Adhem's name led all the rest.

Leigh Hunt

Acknowledgements

Thanks to my brothers: Paul, Philip, David and John for reading my manuscript and writing forewords. They have always been, and still are, part of my life.

Thanks to Pauline Ling who talked about many of our memories during our long friendship.

To Maggie Silver for her encouragement to keep writing.

Many thanks to Jim Greenhalf for his amazing knowledge of commas, apostrophes, date formats and other such grammar. His thoroughness at editing made me feel safe with the end result.

Thanks to Sue Roe, for her most useful comments on the manuscript, and advice with the publishing process.

Thanks to Derek Brown and Jackie Maidment for the design and layout of the book, and getting it to print, also for liaising with others involved in the publishing process which was all new to me.

Introduction

My mother was in my head for pretty well every day from the age of ten until shortly after she died over fifty years later. I used to think that I was the only daughter in the world who didn't relate well with her mother. Of course I did learn that was not the case, but the emotional conflict stayed with me. Near the end of her life Mum came to live with me and I felt the need to let my brothers know that the relationship between my mother and me was not the same as the relationship between each of them and 'their' mother.

In 1978 my father wrote in a letter to his Quaker friend saying *'several years before I actually met my wife, I prayed that God would lead me to the person most suited to me, and hoped that our children would be guided and blessed in their way of life. This prayer has been wonderfully answered.'* Both my mother and father sought to do good in their world. They had strong Christian values. Mum helped people on a local network whilst Dad was more global and concerned about world events. Their religion and arguments confused me and my story includes a resultant mental breakdown. I never married or had children, but when I was fifty I moved house with my great friend Ken who overcame alcoholism.

Hanging in my kitchen is a copy of brother David's portrait of My Parents. To me it illustrates exactly how I saw them. Mum is alert; she has been waiting for us to arrive and now gives her full attention. She has a meal ready and the bed aired. Dad was busy, so as he sits to be painted, which he certainly wishes to do. He is reading about his current concern, maybe some war or an art catalogue. He is less bothered about time or the length of our stay. When David stops for a break he will probably offer his critique — and advise him to stop smoking.

Working as a nurse and midwife, then as an acupuncturist and herbalist, forced me to see life in the raw: health, disease, normal and abnormal. Nursing in Africa, I was privileged to see people with hardly any worldly possessions who were mostly happy and content.

One always watching and waiting, the other always reading, pondering: David's painting: *My Parents*.

Deafness forced me to become a loner. It made me think more.

My four brothers have always been around for me and for each other, even though we live thousands of miles apart. They are included in the book as part of my life.

My mother lived with me or nearby for her last seven years. On the day she died in 1998, I was sixty-three years old. My new computer was delivered with Internet access on the same day. It was a new start in my life.

As I grow older, I feel surrounded by good energy; sometimes I know that what happens to me is beyond my conscious choice. It is the good energy or the God that is everywhere all the time. I often feel the need to thank this 'power greater than me'.

I feel very fortunate that my life has been full and exciting, despite my early questioning of Mum's religion.

The reason I have written this book is because I had so much material: my mother's diaries and my letters home that she kept; Dad's clutter of letters and some of his posters and general memories; Ken's diaries and my own collection of things I didn't throw away.

It seemed as though it was something I should do.

Five Forewords

From Philip, two years older than me, an engineer who lives in Australia.

I was really thrilled that Margaret asked me to write a foreword for her book. I have known Margaret since she was born, her being my little sister, in fact the only sister in a family of four boys. Little did we know at the time that being the only girl in a male dominant house, run by a strictly Methodist mother with inconsistent rules and expectations for us, would bring anguish to young Margaret's life.

I realise now that my Mother had the ability to instil deep guilt and inadequacy in those not hearing the call of God. I was always pretty strong-willed, it did not affect me and so I did not see it.

I quote from the passage Margaret wrote about her time in Australia:

My letters home were totally devoid of religion. Although I always filled the space of those blue aerogrammes with fairly small writing, they were probably descriptive rather than emotional. I tried to keep them newsy and interesting and to give no clue of my concern over the religious connotations written by Mum. I was twelve thousand miles away from her, but I was feeling invaded again in my mind.

Why did Margaret have to go into a mental clinic? Her best friend Pauline said that she lost sight that life was worth living; therefore why was she saving lives and bringing babies into the world?

During that time her doctor asked me about my parents and I explained that my father was quite unusual being a Conscientious Objector, anti-smoking, ban the bomb etc. whereas my mother was a very religious woman who, in my opinion, was quite the perfect Christian. The doctor said: 'Hmmm funny, Margaret has exactly opposite views. Your mother is all about control and your father is easy-going.' Hence, the title of this book.

Being a nurse Margaret shared her passion for helping others, travelling the world to help the sick and needy. It was partly due to her glowing descriptions of Australia, whist on one of her expeditions, that my wife Mary and I and our young daughter Beverley, packed our belongings and migrated there in 1961. One of the best decisions we ever made. We worked hard and it paid off. Eventually we were able to open our own business which was very successful, becoming the largest tanker manufacturer in the Southern Hemisphere. This is where our extended family of twenty now lives.

Through reading this book others, who have shared similar haunted pasts, will not only see a route to enable them to move forward in their minds, but to learn to flourish. I am proud that Margaret has been strong enough to 'tell all' as she sees it.

I feel confident that, through reading this book, people will understand why Margaret's life is what it is and how siblings' relationships with their parents shape their lives.

Congratulations Margaret.

Philip Hockney OAM (Medal of the Order of Australia)

From David, two years younger than me, an artist, lives in UK and USA.

The book is very good. It is a lot about deafness, which I don't think Mum knew much about. She always had very good hearing and didn't really understand what happens when one loses hearing; it's not just volume, it's clarity as well. Even with my hearing aids I can only listen to one at a time; if there are other people talking in the room I just get one sound, and I just want to leave. I can't really stand it.

I can see in Zambia they wouldn't have cared much about your deafness; just getting nurses there was what was important. I don't have much social life now, but I manage, and anyway painting was what I always liked doing and I'm still at it.

From John, four years younger than me, a story teller in Australia

We never know what is happening inside others at any given time, yet we make assumptions without knowing the truth. I have always felt for Margaret from the first time I had any realisation of her position in the family.

Like Margaret, my relationship with 'my mother' was difficult, yet I can recall inspirational times when Margaret and I walked together on the canal embankment from Apperley Bridge to Kirkstall Abbey, chatting as if there were no tomorrow. Margaret impresses how she coped with her deafness, moving on to learn new knowledge to carry her through life. Eager to learn and be challenged. Her book tells her story — I feel saddened at the times I could have done more had I known.

As I say, we never know what is happening inside others at any given time unless we are prepared to share it with those we love. I'm glad you wrote your story Margaret.

Mine will be different.

From Paul, four years older than me, a retired accountant and Bradford Liberal Party councilor and former Bradford Lord Mayor, who lives in Yorkshire.

Makes good reading, but my mother was not your mother.

Although I always found her wants were more than her needs.

From Pauline, friend since 1953.

Margaret and I have been friends and working colleagues through what seems five life times. We first met at the time of Queen Elizabeth II's Coronation. We were starting our three-year nurse's training at St Luke's Hospital, Bradford. We then went on to midwifery training; part one in Bradford and part two in All Saints Hospital, Chatham, Kent and completed our training together. After a short period doing home deliveries we left for Exeter, Devon, to undergo the training course for the Queen's Nursing Certificate. We learnt to ride motorcycles (BSA Bantams) and progressed to become car drivers.

Then we moved to a village in Devon where we shared a bungalow and worked a double district in which we combined general nursing with home deliveries. We both had Ford Popular cars for work and many visits from family members.

The next move was to Australia, then together to New Zealand where we were introduced to Maori culture and were nursing at Te Puia Springs Hospital which had the first Maori matron.

We separated when I returned to the UK and Margaret moved back to Australia. When Margaret returned to Yorkshire we met up again, both working in Harrogate and sharing a flat. In 1966 we went to Zambia together. You could fill a book with our African experiences.

I often went with Margaret on our days-off to visit her parents at Hutton Terrace. I was always made most welcome and Mrs Hockney provided a lovely tea. Her Yorkshire parkin was particularly fine. I met all her brothers on various visits

For years I have watched Margaret become herself, as you might say. She started out as the only girl in a family of boys. Shy and unassuming, she gradually became the person she is today.

This book is a chronicle of her struggle to find her true self and remain true to it.

Pauline Ling

1 Laura and Kenneth

I was going to begin with my mother telling me to never get married but it would be better to start with my parents and how they met.

In the beginning was Laura. My mother was born Laura Thompson on December 10, 1900, the fourth of five children: Rebecca, Jane, Annie, Laura and Robert. Robert and Annie both married and died in their sixties. Jane and Rebecca remained spinsters and died in their eighties. My mother lived until her 99th year — until the end of the twentieth century. Her parents were both officers in the Salvation Army but became Methodists after they were married because the Salvation Army had restrictive rules about married officers working together.

Laura always spoke of a happy childhood in Bradford, going for walks and gathering wild flowers. She would visit relatives in Norfolk by train or on horse and cart. She and her three sisters joined the local Methodist Mission at Eastbrook Hall at the bottom of Leeds Road, a short walk from where they lived. Laura was forever trying and failing to persuade her brother Robert to join them. The Methodist Mission was extended in 1903 to accommodate two thousand people — five

A family affair: the Thompsons. Left to right: Laura, Grandma, Jane, Robert, Rebe, Grandad, Annie.

Wedding of Laura and Kenneth 1929.

hundred more than previously. It was usually full because, along with

the religious services, the Mission offered many social activities to suit all ages.

Laura's Mum and Dad had a double-fronted shop on Leeds Road. On one side her father sold second-hand furniture and bric-a-brac. On the other side her mother sold home-made baking and preserves. Although not rich they were happily employed and open all hours selling the commodities that people needed.

By the time Laura was in her twenties she was totally besotted with her religion at Eastbrook and felt greatly honoured to be superintendent of the Sunday School. Her diaries tell how she got upset thinking that her actions or words were not in accordance with those of Jesus. There were sixty or more children, aged five-and-over at Sunday School in the morning. In the afternoon there were another few dozen beginners aged under-five. Laura took this post of superintendent very seriously and had a vision of working as a missionary, caring for children in a remote part of the world. She thought that would be her calling from God.

There were Sunday school teachers working under her. In March, 1926, she was sent a new teacher by the name of Kenneth Hockney. He seemed very promising and good with the children. Six months later, after visiting her best friend Doris, Laura wrote in her diary:

Doris let out a secret thought that Kenneth Hockney and I are suited to one another. I'm sure she is quite off her horse this time.

Nonetheless, Laura noticed more of Kenneth, a smart young man also involved in many departments of the Eastbrook Mission. On chapel outings and rambles he always had a camera with him. He would take photos of Laura and her friends and slowly a romance developed. They had happy memories of such a trip to Bolton Abbey.

As well as being a relief Sunday School teacher for Laura, Kenneth was a Registrar of the Children's Services, an evening religious service for poor children in the industrial neighbourhood of Eastbrook. Kenneth and other officials were given the right of entrance to the homes of these poor children in order to give a helping hand and encourage families to attend morning service in the main Eastbrook Hall chapel. He was on the council of the Eastbrook Brotherhood whose motto was, 'For God and my brother'. Efforts were made for the spiritual, mental and social improvement of the men of Bradford.

Never far from a book, a newspaper or a photograph: Kenneth 1925.

Kenneth was also involved in fund-raising for foreign missionary workers and he would take leaflets round the local public houses inviting young men to join him. He saw how alcohol could strip fathers of their family function and joined the Independent Order of Rechabites, a temperance society. Both he and Laura remained teetotal all of their lives.

Kenneth was born on May 19, 1904. He was four years younger than Laura, so she probably looked upon him as subordinate. During a short courtship Kenneth was not forthcoming with his marriage proposal, so Laura asked her mother whether it was all right for the girl to pop the question. Her mother suggested that Laura should write a letter to

Kenneth describing her feelings. He was delighted and reciprocated. They became engaged and planned to share their love forever. Kenneth's mother was not too happy about the engagement. He had been giving her one pound a week from his wage, which was only three pounds a week. She was reluctant to lose this much-needed financial addition to her housekeeping to feed and clothe Kenneth, his brother Willy and three sisters, Harriet, Lillian and Audrey. His parents were not interested in religion and left Kenneth to his own pursuits. He enjoyed art and photography. If the 1914–18 war had not invaded his teens he would have studied both.

Kenneth's conversion to Methodism by the gypsy evangelist, Ronald Smith took place at Eastbrook during an evangelical meeting.

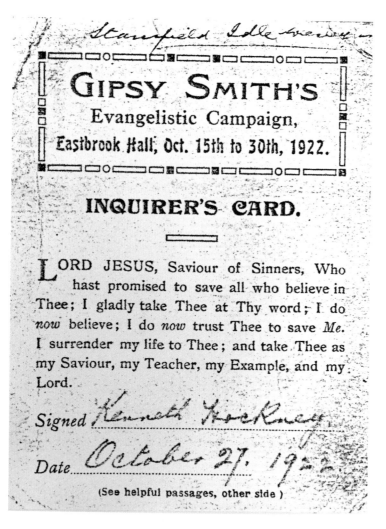

Smith, the gipsy king, converted Christian.

Stanfield Idle

GIPSY SMITH'S
Evangelistic Campaign,
Eastbrook Hall, Oct. 15th to 30th, 1922.

INQUIRER'S CARD.

LORD JESUS, Saviour of Sinners, Who hast promised to save all who believe in Thee; I gladly take Thee at Thy word; I do *now* believe; I do *now* trust Thee to save *Me*. I surrender my life to Thee; and take Thee as my Saviour, my Teacher, my Example, and my Lord.

Signed *Kenneth Hockney*

Date *October 27. 1922*

(See helpful passages, other side)

Kenneth age 16
in the warehouse
of Stephenson
Brothers.

Fast forward to 1975 when Bradford's *Telegraph & Argus* evening newspaper, as it was then, reported on the persecution of gipsies. Dad wrote a letter to the editor:

I am very sorry about the persecution of gipsies. I well remember the famous Methodist evangelist Gipsy Smith who conducted many revival meetings in Bradford during 1922 in Eastbrook Hall: Gipsy Smith was here for one month and must have made very many thousands of conversions to Christianity in Bradford alone. I attended his meetings:

Grandma
Thompson and a
little girl called
Margaret 1938

the Eastbrook Hall was packed with men and women at every meeting, with the seating capacity then at over two thousand. At the Eastbrook Brotherhood meetings on Sunday afternoons, Gipsy Smith spoke to over two thousand men only, at each meeting. They were splendid Brotherhood meetings.

Gipsy Smith's nephew was the Gipsy Methodist Minister, Rev. Bramwell Evans, well known then as 'Romany' of the BBC radio broadcasts about the countryside, birds and nature. He also wrote books on nature. Thank God for that gipsy family. They are worth remembering.

(above)   In the arms of grandma: Paul, Philip, David, Grandma Hockney and me, 1938.

(right)   Country ramble before evacuation and World War 2: Paul, me, Mum, David and Philip in 1938.

Kenneth was the only one of his family to attend regular worship and have strong Christian beliefs. In 1918 when Kenneth was fourteen he left school to earn money to help his mother. He worked first as a telegram boy at the post office and then became a clerk for a firm of dry-salters called Stephenson Brothers.

They had a massive chemical warehouse built in 1881 for the manufacture of dyes and colourings, which they sold to wool textile mills across Bradford. They also made soaps, polishes and lubricating oils. These goods were sold in their retail shop where Kenneth worked as a finance clerk. His wage of £3-a-week remained the same through-out the twenty-odd years that he worked there. How on earth he managed to give money to his mother, pay for his camera equipment and still save enough for a deposit on a house, I can't imagine. He must have been a prudent saver to afford the mortgage on the terrace house in Steadman Terrace, not far from Eastbrook Hall, where he and Laura started their married life on September 29, 1929. They bought furniture from her father's second-hand shop and paid him back in weekly instalments.

They praised God in thanks for their first-born son Paul, born in May, 1931. Philip followed in August, 1933. Laura came to believe that family life was God's calling after all, not the solitary life of the missionary abroad she had thought was her destiny; but children to nurture with a husband and teach truth and goodness. A daughter Margaret, that's me, was born in 1935 and another son, David, in July, 1937. Mum felt that one more girl would complete their young family and in 1939 was pregnant yet again — with another boy, John.

By then the world was in crisis with Britain at war with Hitler's Nazi Germany. All men between the ages of eighteen and forty became legally liable for call-up to the armed forces. Neville Chamberlain, Prime Minister at the time, believed that people should have the right to refuse military service on grounds of conscience and could apply for a tribunal to be exempted from service. Dad applied for the tribunal. He was a Conscientious Objector. He was very stubborn about his conviction of 'Thou shalt not kill' and believed the whole idea of war to be wrong. For him, good could not come from evil. Killing was evil. How could he as a Christian be involved in killing people? He was an absolutist, which meant that he did neither military service nor serve the war effort by being a fire warden or helping with air-raid shelters. His beliefs made him unpopular and, to some, coward-like. He became ostracised. Neighbours in Steadman Terrace scorned him and his heavily-pregnant wife.

Mum was booked to have her baby in the maternity department of St Luke's Hospital, Bradford, where her previous four infants were born. But in 1939 the maternity department became an emergency hospital for military casualties. Midwifery staff were sent to Langroyd Hall in Lancashire which was used as a wartime maternity unit. So Mum and we four children were evacuated to Lancashire. First we waved goodbye to Paul and Philip as their train chugged out of Forster Square station. They were dressed in their Sunday best for their first adventure away from home. On arrival at Nelson local people were asked to help accommodate evacuees without any checking of their backgrounds. Paul and Philip were chosen by Mrs Hartley who drove them to their temporary home where they met her husband who worked on the buses. They were very excited at being driven in a car. Two days later on September 3, it was Mum, David and me who were waving goodbye to Dad as the train took us to Nelson. We probably didn't look an attractive choice in the evacuee reception room; but a kindly Mrs Lund and her daughter Janie agreed to take Mum with four-year-old me and two-year-old David. 'I'm expecting,' said Laura, stating the obvious. 'I can see that,' was the short reply. 'Don't worry, you'll be all right.'

Mrs Lund was very kind. She gave us a large bedroom with a bed for Mum and me and a small bed for David. When Mum went into labour her waters broke first and Mrs Lund called the ambulance in the early hours of the morning to take her to Langroyd Hall in the neighbouring town of Colne. John was born at about teatime. After their two-week stay in hospital, which was the norm in those days, Mum and John were discharged. So my brother John was born in Lancashire on October 23, 1939.

We stayed for six weeks altogether before returning home to Dad who had managed to visit us each week. He was not having an easy time in Bradford. Conscientious Objectors were not popular: even some churches, including Methodists, would scorn them. Fortunately for Dad he was encouraged by speeches on the wireless and articles in The Methodist Recorder newspaper by the Reverend Donald Soper, a prominent Methodist soapbox speaker in London who was also a pacifist member of the Peace Pledge Union. Dad needed to find others with his conviction. That's why he joined the Peace Pledge Union.

Dolly cart. John as doll boy.

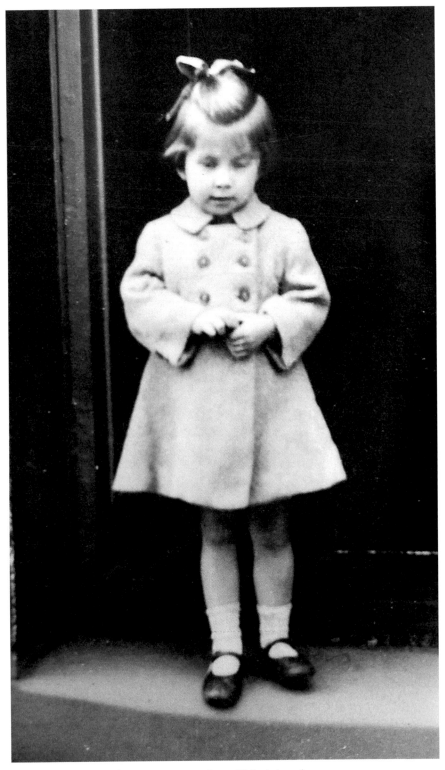

Me on my way to Nelson to get away from Hitler's bombs

Some were Quakers, others were verging on Communism, but Dad

needed all the support that he could find. By the time we came back from Nelson a new and difficult phase of life was beginning particularly for Mum. Dad's new friends rather frightened her. She wished he had done something for the war effort on home ground which might have earned him even a tiny wage. Dad had become very unpopular with workers at Stephenson Brothers, the dry-salters he had worked for since he was young. In spite of his loyal years of employment on £3 a week, he lost his job and had no income.

He had to do some quick thinking. He came up with the idea of buying second-hand prams and dolls' prams and refurbishing them so they looked new. Mum would re-cover the pram hoods and aprons with leather cloth; Dad would put on new springs, cut hardboard for the bodies, use wheels or handles from other prams and then repaint them very skilfully to sell. He bought the old prams cheaply through the articles-for-sale columns in the local newspaper. Sometimes he might have to take a couple of bus rides to purchase them. Being the only girl I got taken along to push the dolls' prams back home. I used to love watching how he repaired and painted them, by hand, using a contrasting paint for the coach lines. They were mostly black and cream or sometimes dark green or maroon with cream lines. I was impressed with the way that Mum stitched the hoods and aprons. She used the old ones as patterns to cut out new pieces from rolls of leather cloth. She had to use strong needles and thick thread and complained the work was hard on her hands. The inside was finished with a new mattress and pillow; she made them look really nice. Dad would then advertise them for sale in the paper using a box number.

When I was five I got scarlet fever. I remember being wrapped in a red blanket and taken to the fever hospital in Bradford for about six weeks. No visitors were allowed inside so Mum and Dad would bring all my brothers and I would wave to them through a window. John would be in her arms; the others sat on a bench in red blazers and white gym shoes. I was very proud of them and looked forward to their visits. The war and another baby put a massive strain on resources. Mum, who never ate meat, decided that if she got half the ration books for vegetarian food she could give us a more varied diet by including extra cheese and nuts. Her sewing skills enabled her to make or alter clothing to keep us all looking decent.

The house at Steadman Terrace was becoming a bit small for a family of seven. We had two bedrooms, an attic and a downstairs room. In the kitchen was a bath with a board over it. The board came off once a week for bath night. We all used the same bath water, which was then used to give a good clean to the outside toilet. We were becoming over-crowded with prams, sewing machine and children. Because of the war there was a lot of darkness. Blackouts meant that all the windows had to be covered with dark curtains before we could switch on a light. There was no street lighting allowed. We had to walk to chapel and Sunday School by holding hands or baby John's pram and feeling the way. Sometimes we had reins on for Mum to keep track of us. Air raid sirens were frequent. Then we all had to squash into the pantry under the stairs or spend the night in an air-raid shelter across the road. One German bomb did serious damage at the bottom of our street. Most of the houses had at least their windows broken, but we, by the 'Grace of God and by prayer' according to Mum, didn't have any damage to the house or ourselves.

Out of the blue in 1943, Dad asked Mum to view a house in Eccles-hill, a north-eastern suburb of Bradford two or three miles from Leeds Road, out in the country. Dad needed to get away from the taunting neighbours. But when Mum arrived at the house he admitted that proceedings to buy it were already in progress and that Steadman Terrace had a buyer waiting. Mum was very unhappy that he had done this without her knowing. It was a shock for her and besides she thought the countryside looked very bleak. Number 18 Hutton Terrace was another terrace house, in the middle of a row of twenty. On her second visit Mum admitted it would be nice to have a bathroom and flush toilet and there was a large garden where we could 'grow our own vegetables', she said. Some of the gardens had hens, one had pigs, and the neighbours assured us that they were all very friendly and shared their produce with each other. The milkman lived a few doors away with giant churns of milk for daily delivery. There were two bedrooms including one of good size at the front with a country view towards Leeds, for Mum and Dad, and a small one at the back, which to my delight would be for me. It had a view of the garden across the terrace. Paul, Philip, David and John were already choosing which of the two attic bedrooms to share.

We had a long walk up to the village and found all the shops that we would need. There was a trolley-bus terminus at the top of Eccleshill to take us to Bradford. We saw two Methodist chapels, the Eccleshill Wesleyan Methodist at Stoney Lane and Victoria Road Methodist. Down the other way there was a goods-only railway station which could be useful for delivering things that Dad needed for his pram business. Two bus routes under the railway bridge in Harrogate Road went to Leeds or Bradford. It was all very exciting.

We moved on May 11, 1943, five weeks before my ninth birthday. We still had to use blackout curtains on the windows, carry gas masks wherever we went and needed ration books for nearly everything; but we soon made friends with other children on the terrace. We found good places to play ball games, hop-scotch, or go for rambles where we could gather bluebells, blackberries or maybe watch tadpoles and frogspawn in the dam at Greengates Woods.

2 Bread and Pilchards

After we moved to Eccleshill I became worried that Mum seemed unhappy. She started to argue with Dad about money and the fact that he had bought this house without consulting her first. I heard them at night. The floors were uncarpeted or had a few threadbare rugs on them so sound carried well. There was a strip of carpet in the middle of the staircase where I used to sit and listen to them when I was supposed to be in bed asleep. Mum usually ended up crying which would upset me as I crept back into bed.

Mum imprinted strong attitudes in me: I belonged to her and should completely believe her and the principles of her Methodist religion. We were all members of Stoney Lane and Victoria Road Methodist chapels and Mum became leader of the Junior Church. She used to visit young families, especially those undergoing hardship, old or disabled people and sick chapel members, offering comfort and support. She was genuinely interested and keen to help folk. She made a register of local people, mostly elderly, who were alone and housebound, and called them her 'shut ins'. She would visit them for chats and take flowers from the garden or hedgerows and, if they were mobile enough, would bring them home to share meals with us and play indoor games.

Dad started to complain that the chapel organ and the hymn singing were too loud, but the preachers spoke too softly. He also disliked the group of smokers who lit cigarettes as soon as the service was over, and thought the stewards were using too much red wine for Communion. He said it should be Ribena or grape juice. He started checking in at churches of different denominations and comparing organs and preachers. And he carried on seeing his Peace Pledge Union friends.

As well as helping people, Mum loved visitors. I never once heard her complain about anyone turning up at the door. All were welcome and offered tea, meals and time. In fact she loved having a houseful of people and encouraged us all to invite our friends home.

There would always be a crowded table for Sunday teatime. She invited some of her 'shut ins' and one of us would help them walk to our house. My brothers would bring friends from Sunday School and fill the room with jokes and laughter. I would help Mum make the tea.

CIVIL DEFENCE

YOUR GAS MASK
How to keep it
and How to Use it
—
MASKING YOUR WINDOWS
—

PUBLIC INFORMATION
LEAFLET

Read this a~
keep it carefull~
You may need i~

CIVIL DEFENCE

YOUR FOOD IN WAR-TIME
—

PUBLIC INFORMATION
~LET   NO. 4

this   and
~it carefully.
~ay need it.

~vy Seal's Office July, 1939

WAR EMERGENC~
INFORMATION AND INSTRUCTIONS

Read this leaflet carefully and make sure
that you and all other responsible persons
in your house understand its contents.
—

Pay no attention to rumours. Official
news will be given in the papers and over
the wireless.

Listen carefully to all broadcast instructions and be ready to note them down.

NATIONAL REGISTRATION
IDENTITY CARD

SERIAL NO.   1

BF 096850

RATION BOOK

Surname *Hockney*. Initials *Kenneth*

Address *18, Hutton Terrace,*
Eccleshill,
Bradford.

IF FOUND RETURN TO ANY FOOD OFFICE		F.O. CODE No.
		EWR - C
		1

There was salad to wash, cucumber to slice and put in a dish with vinegar. I would gather radishes, spring onions, celery and lettuce from the garden and put them in a bowl of strong salty water so that all the caterpillars, slugs or other insects floated to the top of the bowl. Sometimes Mum allowed one egg to be hard-boiled and cut into about twelve pieces and scattered attractively amongst the bowl of lettuce and radishes. I would open a tin of spam or corned beef, or maybe pilchards, then cut and butter two platefuls of bread, often home-made, one brown and one white. A tin of pineapple or fruit salad was opened for afters, topped with Ideal evaporated milk. There was never too much food, but always enough.

Although Mum was vegetarian she was happy enough to cook meat for us. She hated the smell of kippers, but poached them for Dad regularly. I didn't care for them: there were too many bones and such a strong salty taste. Another of Dad's favourites was tripe and onions. Strangely, for a vegetarian, Mum enjoyed bread and dripping, which she made from roasting a small rationed meat joint. Nothing was wasted. She also liked her home-made beef gravy on Yorkshire pudding (made with dried egg), and bread fried in bacon fat. I used to help bake jam tarts, buns, parkin and cakes. Mum was a good inventive cook. Regular favourite meals were cheese pudding, nut loaf, and pudding of battered dried bananas. We got those packs of dried bananas from Nobles, the vegetarian health shop. When we went on picnics and didn't eat all the Heinz sandwich spread or fish paste sandwiches, they would be dipped in dried egg mixture and fried for dinner next day and taste delicious. I didn't like tea, so would have camp coffee, or dandelion and chicory coffee.

Mum and Dad were both about five-feet-two and were quite slim. Mum spoke softly, scarcely ever raising her voice, but used a lot of facial expressions. Her face fascinated me; it was as though I could read her thoughts, even though I may have misinterpreted them. I loved her smiley face, full of cheer, welcome and laughter. That was usually the one when the house was full of family and friends — the more people she was feeding, the happier she would be. Her face was flaccid and mobile. Sometimes, especially when conversing with Dad, she would purse her lips as though trying to hold back tears, but invariably the tears seeped through and she would sob quietly. If she disapproved of anyone's behaviour it was easy to see it in her face, which could feel more scathing than words. She spoke a little louder for the night arguments that I listened to, but I never heard her shout apart from exclaiming, 'Oh horrors' occasionally, if there was a loud bang or something surprised her. Sometimes she would softly hum or sing hymns, a favourite being *What a Friend We Have in Jesus*. There were many more and I knew the words of all of them; I learned them at chapel whilst the preacher was giving his sermon.

Friends and neighbours spoke highly of 'your poor mother'. I never quite understood what was so poor about her; but I was quite a shy and naïve little girl, in the middle of four brothers who all seemed much more important and cleverer than me. I admired my mother though and respected her, but I never felt I could talk to her easily: it was a matter of listen, believe and always try to please. Life was not for sitting around. There would always be some job that needed doing. Washing up, bringing coal in, darning socks, making beds, sewing, knitting, cleaning. As well as Bible quotations Mum was very quick with comments whenever they seemed necessary. She knew a proverb for every occasion and might say for example, 'The Devil makes work for idle hands. Your hands are younger than mine. If it's worth doing it's worth doing well. Put some elbow grease into it. Many hands make light work.'

But the one that really messed up my already low self-image was the supposedly innocent little chorus sung to the tune of Jingle Bells:

J-O-Y, J-O-Y, This is what it means,
Jesus first, yourself last, and others in between

'Sing it Margaret,' she would plead. I tried, but the words upset me; forever putting myself last did not seem right, but that is what I did. I downed myself and hid away in my shell, especially at home. Mum, Dad, aunties, uncles, brothers, visitors and even strangers were all more important than me. I did make friends with Pat at school who lived at the top of Eccleshill. She told me how she liked being the youngest of her family. She was fifteen years younger than the youngest of her five siblings. 'I suppose you are the same with your four brothers, I bet they spoil you,' she said,

'Well not really, but two are older and two are younger, so it's not anything like yours,' I said. Pat's father had a taxi business. There was only one sister still at home, the others were married. Pat already had three nieces.

'Trouble is,' she said, 'my mother is so old. She was forty-five when she had me and I could not bear the thought of losing her. I have promised her that I will look after her forever.'

Next day as I was ironing shirts, I was thinking, that I had never seen Pat ironing, or even cooking. I had long ago learned how to iron shirts: both sides of collar first, cuffs, back, front and finally the sleeves. I moaned to Mum that it was nearly time to go to Guides. She looked at the clock in the way that she always knew what time everything happened and said I could just iron the handkerchiefs and she would finish the shirts later. I liked doing the hankies, folding them into neat piles like sandwiches, some oblong and some triangular. Big ones for Dad, medium-sized for most of us and some special lace or embroidered ones that had been given to me or Mum as birthday or Christmas gifts. Mum was darning socks. As one was darned and folded into its pair, she would put the wooden mushroom into the next holey heel and choose a matching colour of wool. There seemed to be no reason why she said: 'Never get married Margaret.' That was all she said in her soft Sunday School sort of voice. Over the next few years, she said the same thing again and again until it must have had a voodoo spell effect on me because I never did get married.

Both Mum and Dad talked about love, especially that Jesus loved us; but love was a word without feeling to me. Hugging was not the norm in those days. Kissing Mum goodnight was a perfunctory peck on her cheek. Same with kissing anyone: it was a dutiful habit rather than a feeling of any expression. Only on films did I witness closer embraces, but they would embarrass me and I would be glad of the darkness in the picture-house. When I went to Brownies or Girl Guides in the dark about half-a-mile away, Dad would forever remind me to never talk to strange men or take sweets from them. I would run all the way home, but no strange men ever spoke to me. There was one incident upstairs on a bus when I was going to school. A man sat next to me and exposed himself. Not knowing where to look, I stood up to pass him and made a hasty retreat from the bus two stops away from school. I ran all the way in case he was chasing me; when I finally looked round he was nowhere to be seen.

Sometimes after Sunday tea or on special occasions such as Christmas, there would be a fire in the front-room and we would play hide-and-seek, Simon Says, or a similar game which had us walking with a stick — saying: 'Here comes an old woman as stiff as a stump, selling black pudding a penny a lump. You must neither laugh nor cry, but say outright I will,' and offer some sort of challenge. If you laughed or did not say 'I will' you were out. You didn't have to do the challenge — it was supposed to make you laugh.

Dad would often sing his little songs, from music-hall lyrics. We always knew what was coming:

Little Billy Williams found a penny in the garden
One fine summer's day
And as little Billy never had more than a farthing
He shouts hip hip hurray
He toddled to the 'bacconist where cigarettes were sold
And bought a penny packet
Coloured green and gold
Five little fags in a dainty little packet
Five cigarettes that cost 1d (old word for pence)
Five little whiffs underneath his jacket
Willy got pains in his little Maireee
Five little whiffs and in five little jiffs,
He was lying in the tramway lines
With his little face greener
Than the label on his wild Woodbines

He'd forget bits and just hum them, and then he would warn us that cigarettes were not good for anyone.

I had two years at the local Wellington Road Primary School. I enjoyed the lessons and was top of the forty-four students in the class when I finished. I won a scholarship to go to Belle Vue Grammar School for Girls. That is when I started to fall by the wayside. School started in September and all was well until Christmas, 1946, when I was eleven years old. On Christmas Day I was helping to cook the dinner. There was quite a crowd: our family, two of Mum's 'shut in' old ladies and two of my aunties. I didn't feel well, but Mum was not sympathetic at first because she thought I was resenting my domestic duties. It turned out I had pneumonia and was ill for about three weeks. The doctor prescribed me some new drugs called M and B 693 which had been discovered in 1938 as a miracle cure for pneumonia. They were sulphonamides and were big white tablets. That was just before penicillin injections became the cure-all. Being ill meant that I missed the first couple of weeks back at school and I never seemed to catch up.

Being ill in my own bedroom also made me more aware of the arguing when the boys had all gone to school. This was when I realised that, after nearly eighteen years of married life, Mum did not seem to like Dad, which explained why she had told me to never get married. She complained that she was neglected whilst he went meeting his pacifist friends; she asked why he didn't go with her to Chapel anymore and that he was spending too much money on Rowntrees fruit gums and going to the pictures. There were plenty more things she thought were a waste of money. Dad would listen but not say much, as he repaired his prams and painted them whilst she droned on about his faults. My love and admiration for Dad became secret. I couldn't see him as the man that Mum saw: spendthrift, questioning religion, uncommunicative. He always spoke well of our mother and that we should respect her and I thought he was funny and quite clever.

Dad loved the cinema and he used to take us children to Saturday matinees. Mum usually wrinkled her face in disapproval when we went because it was wasting money that she needed for food and clothes. Although I used to join Dad and my brothers when he took us to the pictures my mind would be on Mum left at home doing the ironing or cooking and I would feel so sorry for her that I couldn't concentrate and would often fall asleep soon after the film started. In that way I hadn't really been to the pictures, so whilst Dad and my brothers were broadening their minds, being rapt in the film and living in the moment — often in the American West — I would be hiding in my shell of a blinkered life dominated by trying to always please my mother.

When Mum didn't feel well she would often keep me home from school. This could happen several times a month, usually after a particularly weepy argument the night before — although I wasn't supposed to know about that. Mum, who would stay in bed, had trained us all to make our own breakfast so I would take her a tray of toast and cups of tea. I would be kind and sympathetic because I genuinely wanted her to be happy. Usually I would go to school for afternoon classes. Life must have been hard for Mum when bills were overdue and no money to pay them. Being ill was her way of coping, that and talking to people. She did lots of visiting and chatting. On one desperate day she confided to her mother that she couldn't afford to

buy school clothes for us. Although she did lots of sewing and altera-
tions and shoes were passed down to younger brothers, new clothes
were still needed. Anyway, her mother told Mum's brother Robert (now
married, and never religiously converted by Mum) and he sent her a
£5 note, for which she was amazed and truly grateful. In 2016 that
would be the equivalent of £150.

Meanwhile Dad's method of raising money in an emergency was to
pawn his best suit. This made Mum feel very ashamed. She was hoping
that Dad would get a proper job now the war was over, instead of doing
the prams. Actually the pram business was easier from Eccleshill
because there was a red telephone box about a hundred yards from our
house. Dad would use that phone number in his adverts with a speci-
fied time to phone. He would take a little folding stool to the phone
box at the appointed time and wait for his calls. He started renovating
bicycles as well as the prams. In desperation Mum kept looking for
work herself and finally got a job at a jam factory two bus rides away.
She worked for half-a-day and then next day gave in her notice saying
it was too far to travel. She got paid four shillings and a penny and
remained very unhappy. Meanwhile Dad was applying for jobs and
finally he got one as an audit clerk. He studied by correspondence to
become a qualified commercial accountant.

1948 was a particularly bad year financially. My oldest brother Paul
finished at Bradford Grammar School so needed a decent suit to apply
for work. Philip had two more years at school and was the only one to
wear a maroon blazer, so there was no chance of hand-me downs.
David, two years younger than me, was adamant that he didn't want
to go to Bradford Grammar School, where he was due to start in
September: he just wanted to go to art school. He was bigger than Paul,
so couldn't wear Paul's school blazer, but Mum had made him one from
a neighbour's boy who had just left Paul's class. Reluctantly Mum
applied for grants for school clothes from the Town Hall and within
weeks there was confirmation of clothing grants for Philip, David and
me, plus bus-fare allowance. Mum was soon on her knees thanking
God.

Meanwhile holidays were not affordable, so we children went
farming for a couple of weeks during school holidays. We earned our
keep and it was good healthy experience. We all went to different places
and I mainly did potato picking in Pocklington, East Yorkshire. Despite
the Town Hall grants, Mum still thought Dad was not giving her

War is over, let the good times roll. Front steps of Hutton terrace 1949.

enough money to make ends meet so the nightly arguments continued. Also Dad was getting very involved in making posters for the Campaign for Nuclear Disarmament's ban-the-bomb marches as well as collecting day-old cheap newspapers from the Mechanics Institute Library to keep him up to date with world events. He got Socialist Weekly and The Daily Worker, and Peace News from Peace Pledge Union. He was buying paint and ink and all kinds of paper, calico, canvas and even blackout fabric to make his posters. The house was getting cluttered with this hobby and Mum said he was wasting more money.

It was not long before my thoughts became very mixed up. Religion and loving God were not compatible with arguments and tears. I am sure that these thoughts are what messed up my learning. I was bottling up my confused emotions at home and releasing them by playing the fool and disobeying rules at school, such as not wearing the uniform hat, talking in corridors, chewing bus tickets. What a waste I became, I even had to see the school Child Guidance doctor. Mum went with me the first time, so I didn't tell them why I was being so naughty at school when I was so good at home. I probably didn't know myself at that time.

We were all growing up and making friends. Paul, Philip and David all seemed worldly-wise to me. They told jokes, laughed a lot at meal times, brought friends home and seemed as though they were very clever and popular. Most social events were to do with chapel. There were pantomimes, dances, concerts, and parties. Paul was especially important and had principal parts at these events. As for me, I was becoming very shy and alone. Mum monopolised my mind; I found her seeming unhappiness hard to cope with. She probably wasn't really unhappy — it was just the way I saw it at the time. I am sure that most people close to me never even noticed me. I was nobody to myself: I never expected to have a great social life, nor did I have any ambitions. I had minor parts in the Sunday School plays and pantomimes. I would volunteer to do cloakroom duties at dances. Paul and Philip had started courting and Mum was very clear what she thought about stiletto-heeled shoes, red nail varnish or too much lipstick. So little innocent me put these on my 'what not to do' list at the age of fourteen.

I left school a month after my sixteenth birthday with three GCE 'O' levels: English Language, English Literature and Maths. I had no idea what job I wanted to do, so when Dad's sister Audrey suggested I worked on an accounting machine at Yorkshire Electricity Board that is what I did. There was a room full of girls, each of us working on our machines, a repetitive boring job, but the tea-breaks were fun with accounts of family and social lives much different to my own. A tall fair girl called Susan was leaving to start nursing training. The other girls would taunt her about long unsocial working hours, night duty, battle-axe ward sisters, poor pay, lots of studying, bed pans and diseases. 'Why do it?' they would ask. She had her reasons; but the one that triggered my under-used brain was that she had to live in the nurses' home and had her own room. The home was newly-built and sounded amazing to me. The unsocial hours and wearing a uniform really appealed to me. I was far too shy to express myself socially at home; maybe away from the religious and moral guidance of Mum, I might find my own life.

When I told Mum that I had decided to become a nurse she thought I had been called by God to serve and minister to the sick and needy. She made an appointment with matron at St Luke's Hospital even though I was not yet seventeen and had to be eighteen to start training. Mum must have really impressed matron because a job was created for me as an assistant in the physiotherapy department until I was old enough to start training. I was incredibly shy and hardly spoke to anyone, but I loved the job. It was mostly cleaning physiotherapy equipment, washing bandages and being a general gofer. Those were the days of radiant heat machines, wax baths and stump-bandaging of war wounded amputees. There might be a dozen six-inch-wide wool crepe bandages to wash daily with carbolic soap and dry on the big radiators that heated the department. I then rolled them up again ready for re-use.

I gradually felt less shy and more at ease as I took messages around hospital departments, getting to know porters, cleaners, admin staff as well as the rambling layout of the buildings. One of the porters offered to show me the hospital mortuary where he worked. During the tour I asked him about his views on death. 'Don't ask me,' he said, 'I only work here. My wife thinks I am a regular porter. She'd divorce me if she knew what I really did.' He had been dealing with the dead for many years; I was amazed that he kept it secret. I liked being sent on errands to different departments, especially the pathological laboratory for blood and other body fluid results. There was a room full of microscopes and white-coated workers. I became really intrigued by the cause of diseases. I also got acquainted with the hospital boiler-man. Above the boiler house was a towering chimney that seemed to randomly bellow out clouds of black smoke. Outside were always piles of coal, big shiny black lumps, medium pieces, and smaller chunks of dusty slack. He showed me down below street level where he was forever shovelling coal into a furnace. The work was hot and dusty and at the end of his shift he was covered in coal grime. 'These are three Lancashire boilers and they produce steam at one hundred pounds

Dad's picture 1953 showing my tension at 18.

pressure and use about fourteen tons of coal a day,' he said. Gosh, I thought, twenty sacks in a ton means two hundred-and-eighty sacks a day. We only used about sixty sacks a year at home. 'Yes, they provide steam for sterilisers, autoclaves, cooking in the hospital kitchens, heating the wards and departments, as well as hot water for baths and sinks throughout the General and Maternity hospital and also the nurse's home,' he said.

There were so many interesting parts of the hospital; I couldn't wait to start training. In June, 1953, the big day came. I moved into my room in the nurses' home. At that time there were a lot of West Indians in the UK; the very first Jamaican nurse at St Luke's started the same day as me. Cynthia became my best friend and, of course, my mother was delighted when Cynthia agreed to talk to her Junior Church children about Jamaica. And so started my life away from home, making new friends and learning the foundations and skills of nursing.

3 Carry on Nursing

What a life-changing choice it was. The hospital was typical of its era: a large complex of Victorian buildings based on Florence Nightingale's *Notes on Hospitals*. The National Health Service was only five years old. St Luke's Hospital still had a workhouse stigma attached to it, especially when patients were first admitted; but by the day of discharge they were usually impressed and grateful for their free treatment and nursing care.

My new abode was in the newly-opened nurses' home. In fact it was addressed 'NEW' nurses' home, and it was a super place. There were long corridors full of single rooms with three baths and toilets to each corridor. Four of us from adjacent rooms assembled in the office down in the main hall where two Home Sisters ruled. They explained the house rules, which were also pinned up on the notice board:

Doors locked at 10.30pm. Late passes not available for first two years.

Nightwear not to be worn in public rooms or staircases.

Collect sugar and butter ration weekly in own container, and be sure to hand in your ration book if not done so already.

Student nurses sit in their own area of the dining room, never in the area allocated for Staff Nurses or Sisters.

Never enter the Sisters' or Staff Nurses' sitting rooms.

No talking in the library.

If in uniform it must be complete with cap, belt, apron and black shoes and stockings.

Outdoor uniform allowed during off duty, no apron to be worn under the outdoor navy gabardine. A navy nurses' hat must be worn. Gloves and purse to be black or navy.

Behaviour must be impeccable at all times whether on or off duty, as representatives of St Luke's Hospital.

Mufti to be tidily worn on days off.

Bedrooms must be kept clean and tidy. Bed linen to be changed weekly, and dirty linen left outside the door and will be collected by the maids for laundry.

In this 1954 photo of me in outdoor uniform, notice Dad's sunrise painted at the bottom of the back door at Hutton Terrace.

The maids will clean rooms once a week.

All nurses should have a daily bath and maintain personal health and cleanliness.

Bath must be cleaned with Vim after use.

No jewellery to be worn, and hair should be tidy and away from the face.

Mail can be collected from the Home Sister's office. Look for your surname initial in the pigeon holes.

Any sickness to be reported to Home Sister.

Any general problems to be reported to Home Sister.

When on Night Duty, you will move your room to the night nurses corridor which should remain quiet at all times.

Lots to remember, but it seemed such a wonderful place to live; already we were feeling the friendship of each other in this great new venture. There was Pauline, who had done a pre-nursing course from school; Judy who talked rather posh and came from Harrogate; Cynthia from Jamaica and me. By 8.30 pm we were enjoying a meal of cottage pie and vegetables, followed by semolina pudding and prunes.

The first twelve weeks were spent in the classroom, where Percy the skeleton was suspended in a cupboard and was used to teach us some basic anatomy. We learnt how to cook gruel, make beds, bed-bath a patient, clean mouths, treat pressure areas, and lots more basic nursing care including the importance of keeping everything spotlessly clean on the wards. Urine-testing was a fascinating procedure involving test tubes, Bunsen burners and various bottles of chemical solutions and re-agents. We were warned that watching illness and death could be emotionally difficult; but we were taught how to bite the upper lip whilst supporting patients and relatives with kindness, reassurance and sympathy. It was all very exciting: the learning, the uniform, the belonging to a great hospital team. Matron gave a talk and she was an instant role model, revered, feared and respected.

At the end of twelve weeks we scanned the ward lists for our names. I was to go on Male Medical ward as a first-year student nurse. Suddenly life was a bit frightening. Under the cover of a blue uniform with crisp starched collar, spotless white apron, origami-style folded butterfly cap — having hung up my navy blue cape in the cloakroom

— I presented myself to Sister on the Male Medical ward at 7am on a Monday morning.

Sister was used to getting a new intake of students every three months. Without much ceremony she called the most junior student on duty to take me with her and learn the routine work. The day started by 'cleaning an end'. The two most junior nurses on the ward did this every morning, starting at opposite ends of the ward. This entailed cleaning lockers and bed-tables, scrubbing steel bed-pans and glass urinals, cleaning round the U-bend of toilets and polishing brass knobs on the centre cupboards. I was taken aback by the sputum mug cleaning. These were stainless steel mugs with a hinged lid that had to be emptied and cleaned. They needed a little water pouring in before distributing to patients; otherwise it was very hard to clean them later. The ward sinks and taps were wiped and burnished till they shone; clean huckaback towels were folded fanlike, ready for the consultant to wash and dry his hands. Nurses washed their hands in the sluice, treatment rooms or cloakroom, but rarely in the main ward with its spotless sink which was the exclusive preserve of the consultant. This ward cleaning had to be finished for 9 am and we were hard-pushed to make it.

On Sundays, when the cleaners had a day off, we had to pull out all the beds and do the floors. Tea-leaves from the massive teapots were strained into buckets all week; on Sundays the contents would be scattered on the floor behind the beds. We swept up the damp leaves with large brushes, collecting all the dirt, grime and, we believed, any bugs. This work turned out to be quite fun, although within my training days it became listed as a 'non-nursing duty'. Lots of these menial jobs came under that category when nurses started to campaign and lobby for better pay and conditions; but in 1953 this was accepted procedure.

Patients had breakfast before 7 am: that was the duty of the night staff who would have already done a bedpan round and given bowls of hot water for washing. By 9 am Sister or Staff nurse would write the workbook for the day. First-year student nurses would do the bed-round and feed those patients who could not feed themselves. The bed-round involved rubbing pressure areas with soap and water, followed by surgical spirit and a sprinkling of zinc oxide talcum powder. All the beds had a draw sheet. As the patient rolled over we could pull a clean, cool side of the sheet through to lie on. We straightened the red rubber mackintoshes that were under the draw sheets and left the bed looking tidy and ready for visiting doctors or Matron.

On day one getting round all fifty-two patients seemed likely to take forever; but as the weeks passed the time just flew. We worked forty-eight hour weeks including Saturdays, Sundays and Bank Holidays with no overtime or unsocial hour payments. Actually this suited me: I had a real excuse to avoid chapel or social events. Mum was still complaining of having no money and that Dad did not understand her problems. I spent most days-off at home, shopping or visiting people with her, but was always glad to get back to my own little private space in the nurses' home.

Food was good, but often had

Nursing a career at the age of 18. Me as a first year student nurse 1953.

to be rushed because the dining-room was a five-minute walk from the hospital. One of my favourite meals was morning break. There would be stacks of fresh, crusty bread and dishes of dripping from the home-cooked meat. Sometimes there was beef dripping with lots of brown from the beef'; other times we had pork dripping with delicious tasty jelly. Post-war rationing had almost finished, but butter and sugar still were on coupons so each of us had our own sugar jar and butter ration. There was no fridge for our butter; if you kept it for the week it would be rancid. When fresh butter was issued we would use it quickly, perhaps have bread with butter and jam or Marmite instead of dripping.

Suddenly, at the end of the first year, I was allocated night-duty. By the second week I was in complete charge of a whole ward. Night Sister was available, but she was in charge of the entire hospital. Working with me was one assistant, who was an experienced and mature nursing orderly; but what I was doing still seemed to me a massive responsibility. We learned by experience how to recognise an emergency, deal with it and carry on with the routine. We could be cutting and buttering the bread for breakfast between changing drip bottles, or receiving a patient back from theatre. For us, multi-tasking was all in a night's work. Events were compared next morning when we met colleagues at breakfast. There were lots of lectures to be fitted in before night-duty, on an evening off, or in a morning when night-staff had to stay awake. The teachers were often consultants specialising in their topics. The times that suited them best were invariably 5 pm and 9 am. Often the pen poised to write notes would drop off the page, during that split-second of nearly falling asleep.

Days and weeks flew by. I could put on the uniform and escape from myself, caring only to carry out my duties kindly and efficiently. I would inwardly cringe at some of the illnesses and discomfort of the patients, yet was forever impressed by how stoically most of them coped with these life-intrusions. Using a bedpan in an open ward would have constipated me for weeks; yet these real-life examples of uninhibited bodily excretions were a lesson in a private world of unusual happenings. I supposed there was not much time for embarrassment, the way we doled out bedpans and urinals for all, rolling patients on and off the pan. There were no curtain rails around the beds; instead we wheeled heavy metal screens to surround them for special or embarrassing procedures. The screens, which consisted of four pieces of washable muslin fabric each stretched by a pair of rods, didn't totally hide us. But they did provide a modicum of privacy when we were dealing with catheters, flatus tubes, enemas or any other special procedures. I was in a new world of brave, submissive people.

Bed-sores were known as a nursing crime and should never happen. Sometimes the bed-sore would be a reason or part-reason for admission. However they were caused, they were a terrible sight to behold. Oh the smell, and the gaping hole of flesh over the sacrum, must have been incredibly painful. There would be sloughing and possible infection and always a risk of gangrene. To heal these bed-sores was quite an achievement. Matron did a daily ward round and was always told if a patient had bed-sores.

We had personal visits to matron if we perchance broke a thermometer. Thermometers contained mercury, which had to be shaken-down before use.

Usually there were five or six thermometers on the trolley, which was wheeled around the ward. A thermometer would be placed under the tongue for one minute. After reading and before charting the result, it would be wiped with a clean swab dipped in water, then placed in a test-tube lined with cotton wool and containing glycerin thymol solution to be sterilized for five minutes. Most students would drop at least one thermometer during their training and had to sweep up the balls of mercury, which could be hazardous if swallowed. A trip to Matron with the broken glass followed. It cost sixpence to replace, so we would wait outside Matron's office in a clean apron with a sixpence, a thermometer and some excuse for breaking it. More often than not, Matron didn't take the sixpence but issued a new thermometer and had a chat about our progress. She was highly respected by nurses, doctors and patients alike.

I was lucky in my choice of hospital. There were no really difficult Ward Sisters, although some of them did have the odd quirk such as making barley water for gynaecology patients even on Christmas day, or opening the ward windows every morning for half-an-hour irrespective of the weather.

Patients quickly recognized who they were and supported us student nurses to keep us out of trouble. When one Sister served meals on her ward, she insisted on the plates being very hot. It was the job of the junior nurse to put the plates in the oven before the food arrived in trolleys from the main kitchen. The food trolley would be wheeled into the ward, the junior nurse would fetch the pile of plates in readiness for Sister to serve. All staff were involved with meal-times, so meals were handed to patients as freshly as possible. Many a nurse forgot to warm the plates in time. As soon as Sister put out the food and named the patient — she knew every patient's diet and appetite — we would pick up the plate as though it was hot and rush off with an apologetic look. Patients were used to the subterfuge; it was a source of amusement to them. Sometime it worked in reverse. Pudding plates were hot and the pudding was ice cream. We had to shift those plates double-quick before Sister saw the ice cream melting.

Most of us students would go to Jerome's photography studio and have a sheet of forty-eight poly-photos taken. We would then swap them around so we had memories of each other.

Jobs for Saturday afternoon or Sunday included cleaning trolley wheels and tidying the lotion and potions cupboards. The lotion

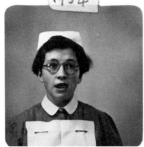

Smile please 1954.

cupboard for 'external use only' was like an artist's palette: gentian violet, Prussian blue, lotio rubra (red lotion), pink calamine lotion, acriflavine (yellow), potassium permanganate (purple), lead lotion, kaolin for poultice, and soft green soap for enemas. Oh, and that wonderful smelling tar-coloured Glycerine and Icthyol solution, nicknamed Glyc and Ick. Urine-testing was a regular and fascinating duty. Benedict's solution in a test-tube with urine boiled over a Bunsen burner could turn from negative blue to green and through to orange for sugar-laden urine. Rothera's mixture could detect three degrees of ketones in urine. To test for albumin we used an Esbach's urinometer, which was a glass tube with marks for R reagent and U urine. It was covered with a wooden case for twenty-four hours, before reading the result. Urine of all new patients was tested. In the sluice there was a rack of test-tubes and a shelf full of chemical reagents. Trouble was, the testing was time-consuming and we could be pressurised to hurry up and get back in the ward. I found the work so interesting and wished I had studied harder at school chemistry lessons.

Early in training we were taught the hygiene principles observed by Florence Nightingale thus:

In watching disease, both in private houses, and in public hospitals, the thing which strikes the experienced observer most forcibly is this, that the symptoms or the sufferings generally considered to be inevitable and incident to the disease are very often not symptoms of the disease at all, but of something quite different — of the want of fresh air, or of light, or of warmth, or of cleanliness, or of punctuality and care in the administration of diet, of each or of all of these.

If a patient is cold, if a patient is feverish, if a patient is faint, if he is sick after taking food, if he has a bedsore, it is generally the fault NOT of the disease, but of the nursing.

We were taught to be aware of nursing the whole person, rather than just the symptoms of their disease.

Working Christmas in hospital was very festive. Each ward chose a theme, and for a few weeks both staff and patients would prepare decorations out of anything they could find and from a big box of decorations from previous years. We made streamers and paper chains with glue, scissors and coloured-paper, crackers from crepe paper, and there would be a ward 'artist' in charge of managing it all. The artist could be a nurse, doctor, cleaner — whoever had the most creative talent. On Christmas Eve staff in capes and uniform and carrying lanterns would walk slowly around the seventeen hospital wards of near eight hundred patients, singing carols, always starting on Children's Ward with Away in a Manger. First thing on Christmas morning around 6.30 am, before reporting on the wards, we assembled outside Matron's house where she and her assistant lived, and gave them a rendering of Christians Awake. They were already awake and came out to greet us. On Christmas Day everybody was on duty and would inspect the other wards. In the afternoon the wards were open to visitors who brought their gifts to patients and staff. Of course, Mum never missed that opportunity to see me at work.

It was great working with colleagues at St Luke's. There was a semi-freedom, but I was always aware that Mum wanted to know what I was doing every day from morn till night. I did not want to share my life that way, so guilt set in. I was not all that bothered about passing the exams and in fact failed the first finals attempt — passing the second time round. However when I chose to learn midwifery, I decided to see how well I could do if I put my mind to it. So far in life, I had not taken any learning at school or nursing seriously. I think this was because Mum had lined me up to be her helper: boys were for earning money. I found out recently from her diary that during my second year of training my mother got a job as a nursing auxiliary on night duty. The job was for Friday, Saturday and Sunday nights; but she said she could only do the Friday and Sunday so she could get to chapel on the Sunday morning. Thank goodness Matron got to know about her appointment and called her to the office. Matron thought it was not a good idea and could be embarrassing for me. She also said that there was an applicant prepared to do all three nights, so Mum had to finish after two nights. Mum had told matron she didn't think that I would have minded. My God, how wrong she was. I would have been very upset and probably left there and then. Nursing was my private place.

She was still complaining about Dad and lack of money, so in March, 1955, I moved out of the lovely nurses' home to live back at home so I could contribute to her income. I gave four pounds in advance for the first month. In 1953, twenty years before decimal currency, £1 was worth nearly twenty times as much as it was in 2016. My salary was six pounds three shillings and fourpence a month, so I had scarcely any money left to spend. Laddered stockings were forbidden, so they were an expensive item. When I was on night duty I left for work at 7 pm and got home about eight in the morning. It worked all right, but living in the nurses' home had been more peaceful.

Things were busy at home. Paul was engaged to Jean, from chapel, and they were looking for a house as they planned to get married in September. Paul was studying accountancy and was a Local Methodist Preacher. Philip was in Cyprus doing his National Service in the Army, but was on leave for a few days.

He was studying engineering. The day after I moved back home, David wanted to go to London because it was the last day he could enter lithographs in the Royal Academy. Mum only had £2 or forty shillings left to offer him. He said thirty-five shillings would be enough. Mum, Dad, Paul and David were busy until 11.30 pm, framing, packing and labelling. There was no suitcase big enough to carry his pictures, so Mum sewed a strong bag for them. Next morning David was on the train to London at 6.30 am. Twelve hours later, when he hadn't got back home, Mum and Dad were getting worried. At 8 pm he phoned from Grantham to say he had not got enough money for the train. Dad rang Grantham station and explained that payment would be made; the station master promised to see that David got the next train home, which was midnight. He arrived back in Bradford at 5am. David told Dad that if he had not phoned the station, he would have been okay hitch-hiking. On August 11, 1955, Mum wrote in her diary:

decide it is time David did some sort of part time job — I think it would be better for him and me. He is painting pictures for September hoping to submit to RA. But still has plenty of time to work I think.

John was in his last year at Carlton Grammar School.

It certainly felt good to get the letters SRN and be a State Registered Nurse. The blue uniform was discarded for a mauve one and, for a brief

Philip, Mum, me, Dad and David.

few months, I became a Staff Nurse. My colleagues were making decisions what to do next. Some stayed as Staff Nurses with a prospect of eventually being Ward Sisters at St Luke's. My Jamaican friend Cynthia was a very popular nurse. She met and married a local boy —

Cynthia and Cyril Wood take the plunge in 1956. I am second from right.

Cyril. They had a lovely wedding in which all my family was involved. Matron attended, along with many nursing colleagues. Cynthia and Cyril then went to Jamaica for a few years.

Some of our group went travelling abroad and some went into the armed forces: the world, it seemed, was our oyster. When I applied to do midwifery, I was having a vision of escaping from Mum into a bigger world; trying hard to get the qualification was worthwhile.
Four of us decided to do Part One Midwifery training at St Luke's Maternity Hospital: Pauline, two twin sisters from Ireland and myself.

4 Deliverance

In 1935, when I was born, St Luke's maternity department was part of the General Hospital; but during the 1940s the facility became St Luke's Maternity Hospital in its own right. As well as the four of us from St Luke's General there were nurses from all over the country. Nearly thirty of us were Pupil Midwives. It was a busy hospital delivering nearly three thousand babies a year, so we had plenty of practical experience. It was a six-month Part 1 course with an exam on completion. Part 2 would be another six months of separate training. Even after three years General Training, I was still a bit naïve about babies and pregnancy, but I soon discovered how much there was to learn about the subject.

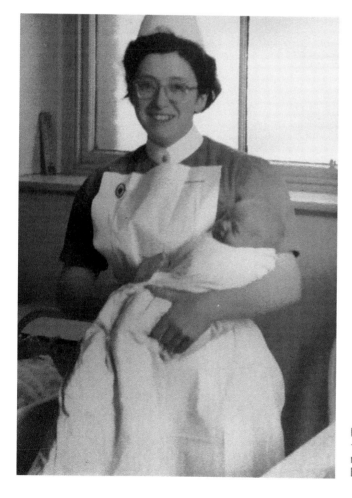

Pupil midwife
1957 at St Luke's
maternity hospital
Bradford.

We learned about the physiology of mothers, the developing foetus and newborn babies. In those days twenty-eight weeks of pregnancy was the marker for a viable premature birth. In the classroom we had a seven-pound baby-sized rag doll stuffed with sawdust. It had a sutured head so we could feel the lines and fontanelles — soft spots — and learn all the measurements of whatever part of the head was presenting first. A knitted placenta was attached by a knitted umbilical cord. Along with a life-size model of a pelvis, we spent many hours delivering that doll through every likely position, including anterior and posterior head positions, breech, prolapsed cord, and to know when the head was safely engaged in the pelvis. Mechanisms of labour were learned by heart so we understood about breech births and other abnormal presentations. We had plenty of laughs, although working out real positions on the mums in antenatal wards was not so funny. There were test papers to hand in every week to make sure we understood the lessons and the practical work.

We witnessed lots of complicated deliveries because the norm was to have baby born at home. The mothers who were booked for hospital delivery had some sort of potential problem and had been advised that they would be safer to have hospital facilities available. Fortunately there were plenty of normal births, so we pupils had good all-round experience. The first normal delivery that I watched was by Night Sister at five o'clock in the morning and it was wonderful. There was just Sister and me and the mother-to-be. It was all so natural and resulted in a little six-and-half-pound baby girl.

Incubators were very expensive; we didn't have any when I trained. Instead there were heated rooms, known as the hot and cool nursery. The advantage of the hot nursery was that the baby could be naked, had unrestricted movement of limbs and breathing, and could be easily observed. The temperature was kept constantly between 80 to 90 degrees Fahrenheit; the humidity at 60 to 70 per cent. Humidity was measured to check loss of weight through perspiration. Any baby weighing three-and-a-half pounds or less would be immediately taken from the mother to the hot nursery. The cool nursery temperature was between 65 to 70 degrees Fahrenheit, and the baby was clothed. This was used for babies under five pounds but over three-and-a-half pounds.

Working on premature baby ward was a very hot task, like going through a Turkish bath. Each baby had his own equipment tray of swabs, eye lotion, olive oil for skin care, feeding utensils; there was a special nurse's gown for each baby. They were treated as sterile entities especially in the hot nursery where they were handled as little as possible. We had to have a calm environment, without random movements or bright lights, and had to be alert for any signs of failing to thrive. A high-pitched scream, for example, could indicate cerebral damage. Babies were fed through a gastric tube with expressed breast milk carefully measured according to their weight.

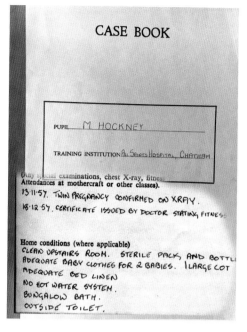

Suitable for home confinement Chatham 1958.

To this day I remember calculating how many calories a baby needed in twenty-four hours — fifty calories per pound of body weight. Breast-feeding was seriously encouraged. A baby weight chart would assure a mother whether her milk was adequate. There should be a slight downward curve in weight, followed by a gentle but constant rise during the ten-day stay. Powdered milk was mainly NDM (National Dried Milk), which was free. We were still using post-war ration books.

Six months flew. Apart from a few pupils who dropped out, we all passed the Part 1 exam. I actually excelled myself by winning a trophy for being 'The best pupil midwife of the year'. The twins from Ireland returned to their hometown. Pauline and I had forged a firm friendship and together would learn Part 2, becoming fully-qualified midwives. We decided to move away from Bradford. As a result of sticking a pin in the map without looking, we chose Chatham, in the garden county of Kent.

We spent the first three months of Part 2 at All Saints Hospital, a dreary relic from the workhouse of Charles Dickens' days, at the top of a long walk up Magpie Hall Road. As well as caring for mothers and babies, we were instructed in the importance of the book-keeping and keeping records — the legal documents for a practicing midwife. Everything about the patient, from ante-natal, labour and post-natal, had to be written down in clear handwriting. There were forms to be sent to the local Medical Officer notifying the birth. Also we had to

Prize-giving 1958. The midwifery trophy is mine.

notify if we had laid out a dead body — this could happen to a midwife who was also district nursing — or if we had a mother with puerperal sepsis, or a baby with ophthalmia neonatorum — yellow discharge from the eyes. There seemed to be loads of things to notify.

The second three months were the most exciting. Pauline and I were allocated the same teaching midwife, Miss Pye, and shared a room in her house along with her school-mistress sister and terrier dog. The midwife had to witness our delivery and management of three home confinements before we were left to cope alone. It was a busy area and within two weeks she had witnessed our three deliveries. We were ready to go it alone.

We each had a register of patients and a drug book to record stocks and usage of drugs. Pethidine and Pethilorfan, which we used regularly, were controlled by the Dangerous Drugs Act, so our book would be checked at intervals along with the balance of drugs in stock. We also carried Chloral Hydrate and Potassium Bromide mixtures, which were helpful to sedate in early labour. For the second stage of labour we had gas and air or trilene. Gas and air was in a box too large to fit on a bicycle; but the trilene was quite a new analgesia that was neatly packaged in a black box which fitted well beside the delivery bag of equipment. We had strong leather straps to secure this gear on the bike. If we needed gas and air, the husband might collect it or Miss Pye would bring it in her car. Hard to believe that we were cycling around with a supply of drugs and syringes, yet never felt in any danger. We were very respected in the area and would cycle blissfully, day or night, to and from our destination.

We taught ante-natal classes once a week at the church hall. On one occasion Pauline and I were alone together and were ready ten minutes early. We had never actually tried gas and air or trilene throughout our training, so decided to have a go. Gas and air is also known as laughing gas — nitrous oxide. Well, did we laugh? Not so much from inhaling through the mask, but from the audacity of trying it. We just found it hilarious. I was first to test the trilene. Wow! My lips felt numb after the first breath and it smelled like a dry cleaner's shop. It knocked me crazy. I was laughing and rolling on the floor with numb lips and couldn't talk properly. I could not do the antenatal class. Pauline led me to a small anteroom to recover; she had to do the class alone.

The telephone at Miss Pye's was downstairs. Pauline and I would take calls in turn. When we needed to go out on visits we wrote the address on a slate. If we both got called out Miss Pye would take the next call. In those days telephones were almost as rare as televisions; personal computers were unheard of. Expectant husbands or some other messenger might come knocking and Miss Pye would always try to be home for them. She would then drive her little Austin car to inform us of any extra visits we had to do. If she left the house empty she hung the slate on the door so that we could be found. We had one day-off a week, and a half-day on Saturday or Sunday. Whilst on duty we were on call twenty-four hours a day.

District Midwifery was a wonderful experience, but acceptable conditions for home delivery were often primitive. We were taught to deliver babies and attend to the welfare of mother and baby in any type of home. This included caravans, houses with no hot water, no inside-toilet or bath, delivery of twins or breech presentations. Because of the large scope of home deliveries we had to be aware of abnormalities such as maternal or foetal distress and understand about the 'flying squad' service, which could be called upon to transfer patients to hospital. Some general practitioners even did forceps deliveries under anaesthetic, expecting the midwife to drip either chloroform or ether onto a gauze-padded metal face-mask. Ether was highly flammable so could never be used in a room with a coal fire, or people smoking. Chloroform was more commonly used as we were told it was inflammable. The anaesthetic powers of Chloroform had been discovered in 1847 by the Edinburgh physician James Young Simpson. There was doubt about safety until 1853 when Queen Victoria gave birth to Prince Leopold, her eighth child, after inhaling Chloroform for fifty-three minutes from a handkerchief. She said it was wonderful, but its safety remained a matter of controversy among doctors.

I nearly had to use the obstetric emergency flying squad. It consisted of an obstetrician and a midwife from the hospital travelling to the house very quickly by ambulance. They were equipped to aid a collapsed mother or baby and would carry intravenous infusion equipment. It was my first twin delivery. The doctor was out on another call, so I was very aware of a possible need of emergency help. Fortunately everything worked textbook-style; I felt great satisfaction at the end of that long night as I greeted two little boys into the world.

Home visiting was a totally new experience. We were reminded that we were always the visitor and must respect every home and its occupants no matter what their status, religion, nationality and the state of the place. I was aware of comparing my own family to those I was visiting. Some mothers and daughters had very close and loving relationships, more like sisters at times, whereas others were more distant: but none seemed to be like my own relationship with my mother. I began to realise what a powerfully emotional effect she had on me. She constantly wanted letters describing what I was doing all day. I wrote dutifully every week or two, trying to write freely, but never really managing it. Her constant need for letters became an intrusion and I felt guilty for resenting her need to know all about my daily life. If there was chance on Sundays, I would go to Chapel, more for Mum's sake than mine. We didn't have Sundays off but there would be a part of the day that those who wished could go to their place of worship.

I couldn't blame my mother, after all I was delivering babies and could see what she had been through to give birth to the five of us. I tried my best to be the loving daughter she thought I was; but she was forever a battle in my head. She did keep me in touch with what my

brothers were doing. Paul and Jean had their first baby and called her
Janine, Philip bought a small house and was to marry Mary in September. David had been working at St Luke's as an orderly because he
was a Conscientious Objector when he was called up to do his National
Service. He was in charge of the Christmas decorations on his ward.
He left there and from October was apple-picking, living in a cottage
in Sussex with two friends. He hoped to get farming work rather than
hospital to complete his National Service. Farming was more his thing.
However, he got work at St Helen's Hospital in Hastings, on a ward
with half-skin diseases and half-medical. He signed up for life-drawing
at Hastings College of Art evening classes. David also told Dad in a
letter:

*If anyone was interested in buying pictures cheap, all those stacked in the
attic can be sold, apart from the 'road menders'. This painting is on a
canvas worth at least £5, so that would be cheap at anything around say
£10. Yes I intend to send a couple of pictures up to the Yorkshire Artists
exhibition and I also hope to send to next year's Royal Academy.*

So John is wondering about joining the RAF? hmm we'll see.'

I was enjoying all the learning and loved becoming a midwife. The
job was very satisfying, especially on the District. Pauline and I now
had ambitions to travel abroad, spurred on by the situations vacant for
nurses in far-away countries advertised in the Nursing Press. Our
teaching midwife suggested we should get a District Nursing qualification first, to have more experience of one-to-one nursing. This sounded
interesting. We applied to train in Exeter.

5 Queer Individuals Doing Nothing Special

Off to London to see HRH the Queen Mother. Pauline and me are 7th and 8th from the right.

We joined a group of six other candidates in Exeter. On arrival we were offered a choice between riding a bicycle or a motorbike. With great excitement we chose to get L-plates and use a motorbike. The fire station was close by. They had their own petrol pumps and service area. They offered to give us free lessons on how to ride the 125cc BSA Bantam motorbikes and service them. The next day I got a provisional driving license and planned to also take car-driving lessons from a lady teacher who gave discount for District Nurses. By July 1960 I had passed both driving test and motorbike test and bought myself a 175cc BSA Bantam. Six of us had our own scooters or motorbikes. We had a wonderful time touring the West Country and beyond.

District Nursing services started in 1859 when William Rathbone, a Liverpool philanthropist and later an MP, employed a nurse so that he could keep his wife at home during her terminal illness. He was so impressed by the help and comfort given that he contacted Florence

Nightingale and, together with his nurse, they developed a school to train District Nurses, initially around Liverpool, which he funded. The training school was a great success and in 1887 was granted £70,000 by Queen Victoria from the Women's Jubilee Fund. A Royal Charter in 1889 named it Queen Victoria's Jubilee Institute for Nurses and was extended all over the country. In 1928 the name was changed to QIDN. (Queen's Institute of District Nursing.)

In 1959 there were not many home visitors. The Health Visitor was almost fully-employed with school clinics and head inspections. Social workers as we know them today did not exist. The 'lady almoner' from hospital could visit the home to assess social conditions and needs. She eventually became known as the medical social worker. Home help was increasing to help mothers for up to two weeks after a home confinement, and to help needy old people. Welfare workers according to the National Assistance Act were making more home visits and were responsible for residential care of the aged.

A lot of our work as District Nurses was with the elderly. Because of the lack of social services, the job could include lighting fires and making tea, even cleaning at times.

The training was four months with an exam, to become qualified members of QIDN Services. Some called it Queer Individuals Doing Nothing Special; but in fact the job and the training were very special. Those who passed the exam had to work a year's contract.

There was a schedule of lectures and observation visits covering a diverse range of potential conditions and services including child care, tuberculosis, mental health, social services, occupational therapy, factory welfare, nutrition, diabetes, environmental hygiene, geriatric care, cancer care — the list went on. Every lecture and visit had to be documented and signed by the superintendent. Added to this were the practical lessons on home techniques of antibiotic injections, insulin injections,

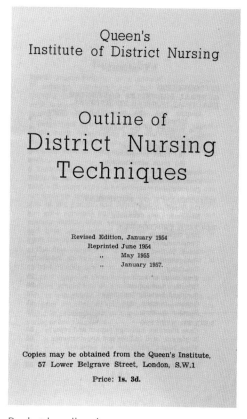

Queen's
Institute of District Nursing

Outline of
District Nursing
Techniques

Revised Edition, January 1954
Reprinted June 1954
     ,,   May 1955
     ,,   January 1957.

Copies may be obtained from the Queen's Institute,
57 Lower Belgrave Street, London, S.W.1

Price: 1s. 3d.

Pocket handbook.

pessary changing, barrier nursing in the home, wound dressing, lifting apparatus, sterilising and care of the 'nursing bags' — all in sixteen weeks.

We had to be aware of helping people stay healthy as well as nursing all kinds of disease problems. We had to gather information about the whole household and their way of life and home environment, to assess where we could help or refer to one of the services or charities.

Our own accommodation while we were training was in three large Victorian-style houses; each of us had our own comfortable room.

We were well-fed in the dining room. Ration books were finally finished with, so after a hearty breakfast we would collect our work lists for the day. We each had our own area with our own round of patients to care for and would make a list of intended work for the next day. The superintendent would scrutinise our lists and might add extra patients from a sick or holidaying colleague, or reduce our list if it seemed too much. Breakfast was at 7.30 am, and half-an-hour later we were all kick-starting our motorbikes and riding full-throttle on our visits. Lunch was at 1.30 pm. The afternoon would usually be free although sometimes we had lectures or learning sessions. We worked again from 4.30 pm until about 7 pm. There would be twelve to fourteen visits in the morning, and six to eight in the evening. A car-driving trained nurse would be on late call to give injections and other late needs.

We started in sunny September, followed by weeks of rainy foggy weather. Motorbike uniform for winter was an oilskin trench coat with a flap for the legs. We were taught the importance of first impressions when we visited our patients. This could be difficult, standing at the door in a soaking wet coat, gloved hand carrying the wet black nursing bag, the crash helmet dripping rain onto the face. Many of the patients or relatives would be ready for us and hang our coats to dry near the coal fire: but there was never time for them to dry properly; we would leave the house wearing a steaming but wet coat, rain still dripping from the crash helmet. We also got sore legs when a wet slippery shoe missed the kick-start pedal. It was not the easiest weather to be mastering the motorbike, but we did have plenty of laughs along the way comparing our bruised legs and dilemmas. Back at headquarters there was a special room for drying sodden trench coats.

Having done midwifery we were at an advantage with some of the home care techniques; but there was a lot to learn in order to have a well-organised daily routine, offering the best possible all round care.

There were no disposable syringes in those days. We gave lots of injections using glass syringes. These had to boiled for five minutes to be sterilised. This was done in a saucepan in the patient's home, kept specially for the purpose. Penicillin was not in tablet form so we might have to visit three or four times daily to give various types of penicillin injections. TB was fairly common, we gave daily streptomycin injec- tions along with tablets taken by mouth called PAS and INAH (Para-Amino-Salicylic-acid and Iso-Nicotinic Acid-Hydrazide). For-tunately I always liked learning new words.

Dressings were regular jobs, we could usually persuade patients and their relatives to keep a stock of home-made dressings. We would supply a roll of gauze, which was cut and folded to the necessary size. These would be placed in an empty biscuit tin and baked in a moderate oven for an hour until they turned light-biscuit colour. Cotton wool would be teased into balls and put into another tin to be sterilized at the same time. As there were no plastic bags for rubbish we recycled newspapers, folding them in a special way to make waste disposal bags. For patients needing dressing changes, we would recruit them into making a supply of these bags. District nursing was refreshingly dif-ferent to hospital nursing.

Pauline had a patient in Heavitree who invited any District Nurse in the area to have morning coffee with homemade Devonshire clotted cream on digestive biscuits. It was not really on my patch, but I did sample this version of morning coffee with a cream tea a couple of times. It was quite delicious too.

I used cleaning skills that I learned in general training. There was an elderly couple living in a dilapidated cottage in my area of St Thomas'. The lady was nearly blind and diabetic and I gave her daily insulin injections. Her husband sat in a dismally dark room at the back smoking his pipe. The front room where I gave the insulin was also the bedroom. The windowsill was full of pots of geraniums, which thrived between the cobwebs, and provided a reasonable view from the out-side; but the whole house was filthy. When a syringe was used daily, as for insulin, it would be left at the house usually in a deep glass butter-dish with a lid. We would put a layer of lint on the base and cover it with surgical spirit. After daily use the syringe and needle would be rinsed with boiled water, then returned to the spirit. Unfortunately the lady became ill and needed assistance with general care such as washing and dressing. Her husband found me a cracked china bowl with a pattern of rosebuds on a yellow background. He had a matching china bucket to pour the water in when I had finished. I asked for soap, flannel, towel and some clean clothes for his wife. The flannel he gave me was grey and slimy and the whole procedure very unsatisfactory. Those china-washing sets were so heavy and awkward to use. Water was heated in a large black pan on the open fire and was never quite hot enough. After a few days of this, I asked the superintendent for permission to do some cleaning. Even when Home Helps were available, many patients were not keen on having one. There were not enough anyway. Permission was granted if the patient agreed. I asked the couple if they would mind me returning in the afternoon to clean up a bit. I am not sure whether they understood my Yorkshire accent, but they didn't seem to mind. I spent two afternoons scrubbing out their two rooms, bringing them a flannel so I could throw away the slimy one. It made the visit much pleasanter and I became fond of the old couple.

At that time SRN was a required qualification for Queen's District Nursing candidates, but soon State Enrolled Nurses were also accepted. They had done a two-year General Nursing course instead of the three years of SRN. A few years later Nursing Auxiliaries were employed as bath attendants and they could help with general care of patients under the guidance of a Queen's Nurse.

There was no time off to go home to Yorkshire until the four-month course was completed, so Mum sent Christmas cake, mince pies, nut loaf and shortbread. I sent Devon clotted cream to her. Most of us were regular knitters, forever knitting cardigans, scarves, and mittens. Christmas gifts for my brothers would often be knitted garments. Asking about sizes was something to write about to Mum. I also enjoyed basket-making and made baby baskets for my two sisters-in-law.

I was writing the regular letters that Mum so desperately hoped for. There used to be two post deliveries then, and she would be forever on the lookout for the postman. She was again asking if I still went to chapel. I replied that neither Pauline nor I went to church very often. We only had alternate Sunday afternoons off, and usually enjoyed a ride in the country, to Exmoor perhaps, or Lorna Doone Valley.

Pauline and I finished Queen's nurse training in 1959, the centenary year of District Nursing. We were invited to a Review of District Nurses

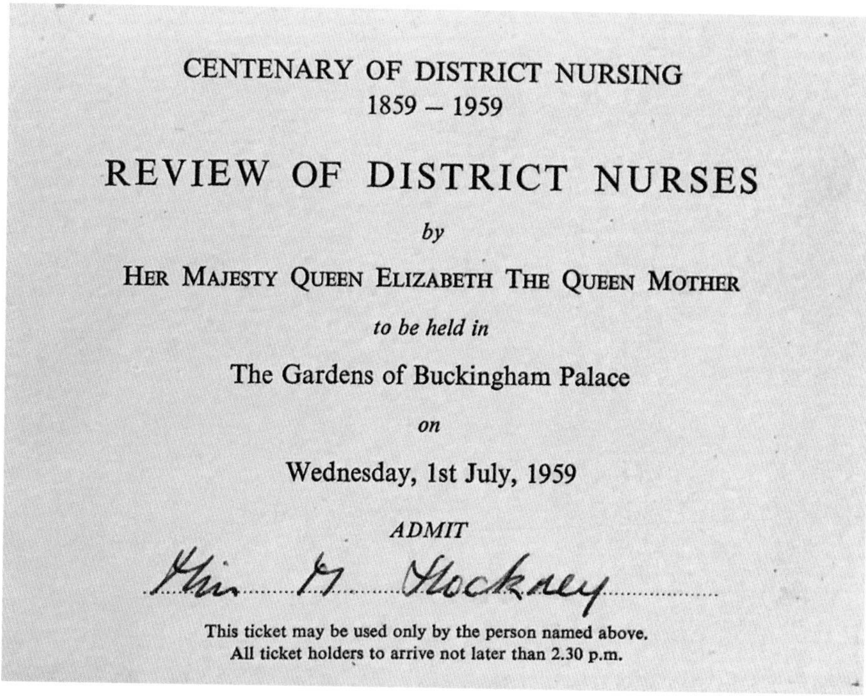

CENTENARY OF DISTRICT NURSING
1859 — 1959

REVIEW OF DISTRICT NURSES

by

HER MAJESTY QUEEN ELIZABETH THE QUEEN MOTHER

to be held in

The Gardens of Buckingham Palace

on

Wednesday, 1st July, 1959

ADMIT

Miss M Stockley

This ticket may be used only by the person named above.
All ticket holders to arrive not later than 2.30 p.m.

Dear diary, big day ahead.

by Her Majesty Queen Elizabeth the Queen Mother in the gardens of Buckingham Palace.

Twenty of us were chosen to go, wearing our smartest uniforms. We travelled by train to London and reached the Palace by 1.30 pm ready for the review at 3 pm. While we waited the Band of the Grenadier Guards played a programme of music. There were crowds of district nurses from nation-wide but we were lucky to be on the front row near enough for the Queen Mother to ask if our feet were aching from standing so long. After the review we had tea at Caxton Hall, followed by a service of Thanksgiving and Rededication at Westminster Abbey. We left London at 11.30 pm and were back in Exeter for 3 am next day. Our patients were eager to know all about our wonderful experience.

When we finished working the contract year in Exeter, we decided to move to a district where we could practice midwifery as well as general nursing. The thought of another winter on the motorbike was not pleasant. We applied for a job in Plymstock and were excited to be given a car each for the job. Pauline had a Lambretta, so we drove her scooter and my motorbike to the new house and then returned by train to collect our cars.

Wearing the Queens
Nurse badges in earnest.

We had a nicely furnished two-bedroom bungalow, with sitting room, dining-room, utility-room for bags and equipment, small garden with a vegetable plot and a double garage. There was a cooker, boiler, and wringer or mangle. Gas fires in three rooms, coal fires in two rooms, also an electric stove and a Hoover. The rent fully-furnished was £60 per year (£966 in 2016). The house was a dream, we were so excited. It was a 'double district' so Pauline and I would work together, fill in for each other and do General and Midwifery. We could even use the cars privately within Devon, Cornwall, Somerset and Dorset for four old pence a mile — just under 5p.

As both our mothers were in need of a holiday, we invited them and other family members too. My mother would be much easier to handle if there were more people around. I was thinking one visit would be worth half-a-dozen letters. My mother was delighted. She wrote and told David and he sent her a cheque for £6 to pay for her fare, telling her that he had just sold a painting for £48. That was a lot of money in 1959 — about £780 in 2016 — when even professional footballers were only on £20 a week during the season.

Pauline's mother and mine spent two weeks with us in March and had a glorious time. I actually enjoyed their company. They did lots of tidying up around the house and garden.

Work was wonderful. We had midwifery patients as well as general district nursing. We also met up with the two local colleagues and the group of doctors in the village. The house seemed to be a haven for mice so we got a large white cat, but he turned out to be a fussy eater. I can recall the days before pay-day when we would buy whiting for the cat and cheaper fishcakes for ourselves.

Mum and Dad came together in June for two weeks. Either Pauline or I drove them to different places every day: the coast, country, shopping — they had a lovely time and so did we. Mum wrote diaries about her three stays with us. Every day was full, trips out, gardening or making things for the bungalow. On our nursing visits we would gather wild mushrooms, bilberries, primroses and whatever else we could forage.

David had a short holiday with us. He had finished his National Service duties in hospitals and at last was a student at the Royal College of Art. His digs in Earls Court had one room with two beds, a gas-ring and wash-basin; he shared a kitchen, toilet and bath downstairs. He said it was a ten-minute walk from College. He sent detailed letters of his day's routine to Mum, same as I tried to do. He arranged to take a job during the Christmas holidays with the GPO, posting mail. He enjoyed his first term and spent almost £20 on paint, staying in college until 10 pm and all day Saturdays working very hard and loving it. In keeping with his pacifist beliefs, he became vegetarian. Vegetarian restaurants were still a bit of a rarity, so he was always pleased to find one. When his letter writing had not been prompt he apologised to Mum:

I know I have been a bit slack not writing, but I am working like a mad man — every night as well (painting).

David and Dad were in their separate ways aiding the Campaign for Nuclear Disarmament, marching, writing letters and making posters.

John had his 21st birthday; I could scarcely keep up with his new jobs and changes of address. He seemed well though.

Paul and Jean were decorating their home in Idle and expecting a second baby. Paul was working at an accountant's and studying accountancy.

Philip and Mary were busy with young daughter Beverley in their little home also at Idle. He was working at an engineering company studying to be an engineering draughtsman.

Pauline and I began to realise that our pay did not go very far. After deducting rent, take-home pay was less than £8 a month. I was still paying the hire-purchase for my motorbike. We had no hope of holidays except the day-trips and visitors. The grass of Australia was growing greener we thought, so we applied for jobs with the Victorian Bush Nursing Association. There were lots of forms to fill and references to get, certificates to be photocopied, vaccinations to check; we knew it would take a few months before much happened. Actually processing our applications happened rather quickly. By September we had secured a job and were told we would fly to Australia early in January, 1961. We gave notice to finish on December 3 and then, to help us afford the uniforms and the money we would need in Melbourne, we returned to my home in Eccleshill to work as midwives in Leeds Maternity Hospital.

We got references from all the places where we had trained and worked and, by January 21, 1961, we had left the snow in England and were on the BOAC 707 to Melbourne. I was so excited at flying that I even made a note of every meal we were offered. Every time the plane stopped for fuel, we would climb out for refreshments and a walk round the airport. We stopped at Frankfurt, Tehran, Delhi, Rangoon, Singapore, Djakarta, Darwin, Sydney and finally landed at Melbourne in the middle of their scorching-hot summer. At every stop we adjusted our watches; I got so confused tying to compare the time at home that I lost track of how long the trip actually took.

6 Down Under

We spent the first two nights in Melbourne at a nurses' recovery hostel. It gave us time to acclimatise to the rapid change of weather and also to visit the head office of our new employer in Collins Street, Melbourne.

Our first post was at Cobden, about one hundred miles west of Melbourne, beyond Geelong. We got there by train. The hospital was only three years old, built in 1958, a busy eight-bedded place delivering about five midwifery cases a month. The rest was surgical and medical. Food was good, grown and farmed on the vast surrounding grounds. We would have chicken for Sunday lunch, killed on the spot then plucked and cooked. The main industry was dairy farming. Most families had horses, cows and a large car. They had a cattle market once a week. Everybody was friendly and offered hospitality and car-trips around the area.

After a few weeks we were on the move, relieving holiday staff. Next stop was the beautiful winter skiing resort of Bright, totally surrounded by mountains and forests. The hospital had eight beds and was almost self-sufficient for food. Flies, mosquitos, bats and kookaburras abounded. Pauline's long hair attracted a bat, which caused a stir for the time needed to extract it.

Life was good. We coped just fine working with whatever happened day-by-day. Two of the most critical events were a car accident with the driver killed and two seriously-injured passengers. The other was a man from the local sawmill who accidentally sawed his hand almost completely off. He arrived with his arm wrapped in a towel. We helped the doctor make a support for his arm and stopped the bleeding. The injury was too serious to deal with at Bright, so the man was airlifted to Melbourne Hospital. Unfortunately his hand had to be amputated completely.

Our third bush hospital move was to Chelsea, a fifty-minute train-ride from Melbourne. The hospital was bigger: it had twenty-four beds, more staff, and was a wonderful friendly place. We enjoyed long walks along the beautiful Chelsea beach, which stretched for miles in both directions, running parallel to the main Nepean Highway and the railway line. We could walk as far as we liked, either two or three hours south to Frankston or an hour in the other direction to Edithvale or

Mum said she didn't get enough letters.

Aspendale. We returned by train from a local station. We would visit Melbourne on days-off and browse round the shops and cafes. We enjoyed toasted raisin cinnamon bread at the Myer department store, or for a cool refreshing drink go up to Collins Street and have a Bloody Mary. As there was no NHS, we joined The Hospital Benefits Association, which cost about £10 a year and would cover just about all medical expenses. I bought a Rabbit scooter, which was a faithful

little bike and I enjoyed being motorised again.

Towards the end of our first year I was happy and thrilled with my new life. We were paid about £14 fortnightly, nearly twice what we earned in England, and I opened my first bank account. The climate was so pleasant that I intended to stay and settle in Australia. Our colleagues were all trained nurses or midwives, with good supporting domestic staff. It was a happy, efficient hospital environment and I was finally feeling the freedom to make new friends and live my life away from Mum — but, oh dear, she kept creeping back into my mind which would trickle with guilt and negativity.

Although I was sending regular letters home saying how lovely everything was, Mum would be forever saying I didn't write enough. I would send postcards between the letters showing the wild life and wonderful views. Mum would say how lucky I was — she never had such opportunity. Was I going to chapel? She wrote religious comments and ended with blessings. She said I was working through God to help the sick and needy.

How could I possibly tell her that it wasn't true? Neither Jesus nor God had ever called me. Praying felt futile and as for chapel, well, there were more interesting things to do. I was not a good actor and terrible at telling lies. I always wanted to tell the truth. Many years later, after Mum died and I read her diaries, I know she had asked Philip, David and John about their religion. They seemed to have managed to answer honestly, although still leaving her perplexed enough to ask her Saviour to help them. Of course Paul, the oldest, was already a Methodist local preacher. Thank goodness that one of us had the true calling that pleased her. My letters home were totally devoid of religion. Although I always filled the space of those blue aerogrammes with fairly small writing, they were probably descriptive rather than emotional. I tried to keep them newsy and interesting and to give no clue of my concern over the religious connotations written by Mum. I was twelve thousand miles away from her, but I was feeling invaded again in my mind.

I don't remember much before the nervous breakdown, but I do remember my bedroom at Chelsea. It was a neat little room that had space for my large portmanteau of possessions: an aluminium trunk with a shelf on the top of a deep cavity. I kept it locked and covered with a plum-coloured chenille tablecloth folded in two. It served on one side as a bedside table and fitted snugly against the opposite wall, acting as a seat beneath the window. That is where I would sit with my head in hands asking:

What am I supposed to do?'

Why am I here?

If you can hear me Jesus, please help me.

Why? Why?

Matron and my nursing colleagues could see that I was in despair. I couldn't sleep with the guilt and turmoil in my mind. I would be tired but not sleepy, couldn't or wouldn't eat, I'm not sure which, but I lost a lot of weight. I told nobody the reason. I felt ashamed. My mother was a good person, who loved us all and only had good intentions. Her handwriting was beautiful, level and confident. Her letters were full of news about family and friends, and her spelling was perfect. She was kind and generous and would help anybody in distress. She hadn't done anything wrong, it was me who was wrong and I didn't know how to handle it. I reached the stage that the sight of air letters made me cringe as I opened them. They were sacred and I looked forward to them, yet they upset me dreadfully. I could not tell anyone.

I struggled on for a couple of months during which time my brother Philip and his wife Mary docked for twenty four-hours in Melbourne on their long sea-voyage to Sydney, where they were emigrating with their two-year-old daughter Beverley. They were on the '£10 Pommy' scheme, £10 being the cost of a one-way voyage with a contract to remain in Australia for two years. Philip believed there would be more opportunity for promotion and maybe self-employment Down Under. Pauline and I spent a pleasant time with them and showed them round Chelsea Hospital. A few weeks later we visited them in their reception hostel in Sydney. For a while I seemed to be getting better, but more letters triggered the guilt, depression and anxiety all over again.

I first wrote about the nervous agitation that my regular doctor diagnosed in the last paragraph of a reasonably newsy air letter to 'Dear all', which included Mum, Dad and John. The next letter on January 7, 1962, was addressed from the clinic to which I had been admitted. It was The Malvern Clinic, for the treatment of nervous diseases. I wrote that I would only be there for a few days, to get my sleep pattern improved; if I could sleep better, then my appetite would pick up.

Otherwise, I assured them, there was nothing to worry about.

Truth was, getting better took nearly nine months.

When I was admitted, Matron sent a letter to Philip which ended:

I think if at all possible you should come to Melbourne and see Margaret. Also I think you will be shocked when you do, as she has lost a lot of weight as she has not been eating — nor has she been sleeping.

At the end of January, Philip Mary and Beverley drove the five hundred and seventy miles to see me. He wrote a long letter to Mum; including:

When we first arrived she was very nervy and burst into tears saying 'I don't know what this is all about. I'm OK really.' We went to Chelsea Hospital to talk with Pauline and matron. Apparently a while since, she got very worried about the reason for life — why are we here? What good is my life? What happens after life? She took up an atheistic attitude. Pauline joined us and we spent all Saturday afternoon with her out in the grounds. She seemed better but still touchy and cried a little when Beverley gave her a big squeeze bye-bye — but that's not surprising cos Bev squeezes so hard.

When you write to Margaret don't give her any advice (Doctor said). Also mum please don't mention religion to her or say you are praying for her as I think perhaps that will set her off again on the 'what is life?' type of thought. I saw Dr Webb the chief psychiatrist and he said Margaret was in a very bad depressed state. He said nobody knows what brings it on. Some people feel really worthless and feel like they have to work like mad as a sort of penance for all their wrong thoughts. He also said that bad depression has a good hope of full recovery. He let us take Margaret out for the day. We went to Chelsea Hospital, then to the beach and then to see the terrible damage caused by the bush fires. Don't worry too much. She will be OK and I'll let you know if anything else turns up.

I was very fortunate. The wonderful caring people and Matron, with whom I worked at Chelsea Hospital, made sure I had the best possible care. That is what I got in the Malvern Clinic, a place for short-term cases where there was a good prognosis paid for by the Australian government. Mum immediately wrote to Matron at Chelsea asking how I was.

Matron replied on February 7, 1962:

Dear Mrs. Hockney,

Thank you for your letter, I will try to tell you about Margaret. I realise that you are so far away that naturally you are anxious about her. Firstly she seemed quite happy and well, but complained of having too much leisure and did not seem able to adjust herself to it.

We suggested various interests for her, but she seemed not to have the inclination or will to take them up. Later she became very depressed and was always trying to find out the reason for everything saying why? Why? Why?

At this stage and under the guidance of a local doctor, she visited a psychiatrist (Dr Whittaker) who gave her tablets and asked her to visit him a few weeks later. On this second visit Dr Whittaker thought she needed further treatment and suggested Dr Webb at the Malvern clinic, but owing to the Christmas period this was left in abeyance.

Also at this time Margaret with friends had a weeks leave travelling by car through to Queensland and then to Sydney. She was very much improved after this trip, when she again visited Dr Whittaker. He thought she was very much better. Later she again became very depressive so an appointment was made with Dr Webb at the Malvern Clinic.

The clinic is a nice quiet restful place, set in lovely grounds and everyone seems very kind. I feel that Margaret is in the right place and under the right care, and when she has completed her treatment, and with the doctors permission for her to resume her normal way of life, I feel that she should be quite well again.

On my visits to her, and also of the staff, we see a definite improvement at each visit. She is putting on weight; the treatment has given her an appetite and is helping her to sleep.

Previous to her visit to the clinic, she was neither eating, nor sleeping well, therefore she had lost a considerable amount of weight.

All the staff there are very kind to her and she does not lack visitors. I am sure it must be a comfort to Margaret to know that her brother Philip and his family are in Sydney.

There are stories of terrible happenings in 1960s psychiatric hospitals, especially the use of insulin shock treatment and ECT

(Electro Convulsive Therapy). I had both of those therapies, but in the gentlest and most humane way. My memory was fuddled for a short while after each treatment. Possibly my recall of childhood is missing, but I don't feel deprived in any way. When I talk with friends and family, my memory seems to hold its own with theirs.

The Clinic was in beautiful surrounds with gardens to walk around. I was allowed to go out into Melbourne, to the cinema, or wherever I wished. The doctors and nurses were kind and civil. I can't remember what I actually said at my weekly interviews with the doctor, but I always looked forward to our talks. Perhaps partly because I was a trained Nursing Sister I had a lovely room of my own which was comfortable and had a window looking out onto a colourful flowerbed. One lot of flowers would follow another — all sizes and colours.

When I arrived at the Clinic I was very agitated, had lost about two stones of my normal eight-and-a-half, couldn't keep still, was sleeping only a few hours at night and had no appetite. Help was certainly needed. The first week I started having modified insulin treatment, in which low — sub-coma — doses of insulin were injected. The idea was to relax the tension and improve the appetite. This was a current treatment of choice to use in patients suffering from physical debility and loss of weight associated with states of tension, generally of a neurotic character. My appetite returned and I was sleeping much longer, so I was able to relax more during the day.

About sixty day patients attended daily to join the twenty resident patients in therapeutic activities. Mum was asking me in her letters what was I doing all day. In April I wrote:

I am much better, but they tell me I am too busy with knitting, stools, baskets etc, but I don't want to sit doing nothing as some do. I am in a very nice single room. Out of the window there are lots of dahlias in bloom. We have early tea or coffee on waking, and toast if we want it. Breakfast is at 8.15am then we are free until 9.30 when the programme for the day begins. A timetable is written up for the week, so we know what to do. We are divided into 4 groups about 20 in each group for the various activities. A typical day would be:

• *9.30am to 10.15: Floral arrangements or puppetry.*

• *10.15: Morning tea or coffee and biscuits.*

• *10.30 to 11.30: Occupational therapy, stools, basket making etc.*

- *11.30 to 12.30pm: Art room, painting, pottery, papier mache.*

- *12.30: Lunch. Groups wash up dishes in turn.*

- *1.30 to 2.30: Games, gardening, debates, play reading or anything.*

- *2.30 to 3.30: Group discussions on any subject.*

- *3.30: Afternoon tea or coffee and cakes.*

- *4.00 to 4.30: Music, dancing, active games.*

- *6.00: Dinner.*

- *9.00pm: Milk drink and biscuits.*

The organisation is very good, the timetable being clearly defined. I have discovered a new word game that I play sometimes called Scrabble.

We also have film shows of psychological problems and then discuss the film. Today we watched 'chronic alcoholism'.

I am feeling quite well, but the tablets make me a bit dopey at times. I get a lot of visitors from Chelsea.

My favourite activity was in the Occupational Therapy room, where I made all shapes and sizes of baskets from willow cane — lined baby baskets, picnic baskets, shopping baskets. I made stools topped with coloured macramé or sea grass, mosaic-topped round tables, a rose-patterned wool hearth-rug, knitting to fill any spare time between these activities. I sewed many dresses for myself and others. To be able to work so fast and create those things was marvellous. My rapid productions so impressed the staff that I had a list of things they wanted to buy from me. I only charged for materials, never to make a profit. Doing this was a real haven for me. I could lose myself in wonderful creative activity, with the bonus of people actually liking and willing to pay for what I made. I promised Mum that she could have the rug I was making.

But I was working too hard, couldn't slow down; so even though creativity was part of the therapy, I had to cut down my time in occupational therapy and spend less time on solitary activities and more time on pursuits such as discussion groups. I can't remember ever talking about my true problem because how could I, when I was my own problem? Most of the other patients were a similar age to me, in their twenties, and the common problem with most was a romantic relationship breakdown or sexual inadequacy. I presumed that I was the only one with a religious mother problem. Romance was nothing to do with me. After all I was never getting married, period.

I still had too much nervous energy. When I got letters from home the depression would hit me again, so I signed a form consenting to have ECT, although they called it electrical therapy. I was told that I would first have a short lasting general anaesthetic and would have only a small amount of electric therapy.

I remember the ECT days quite clearly. It was performed in my own room, on my bed, once a week for four treatments. I had to lie with my head at the foot of the bed; the metal end was removed so my head was at the very edge of the bottom of the mattress. A doctor and two nursing sisters would come in with a trolley. With one nurse each side of me gently holding my arms, I was injected with general anaesthetic — I think it was thiopental — in one of the arms and asked to count to five. I don't think I ever got past three before losing consciousness. I would wake up within half-an-hour. The nurse who had stayed in the room asked me to spit out the black rubber airway from my mouth, then she would make my breakfast of coffee and toast. I would spend the rest of the morning lounging in bed gradually remembering my surroundings. By noon, nurse reminded me that it was lunchtime and up I would dress and join the day's activities.

By May, about five months after I was admitted, I had become very content with the clinic routine and had no thoughts of getting better or going back to work. I was quite all right, out-putting masses of occupational therapy creations but if they needed my bed, I said that maybe I could buy a caravan somewhere and do odd jobs. What I didn't know at the time was all the correspondence being posted about me.

Philip wrote:

I don't think Margaret is any better really, although she is different to what she was before. Last time we saw her she was rather 'lost' and said she didn't know why she was there.

Now she says that she is quite content there as there is nothing else she wants to do unless it is to go into orbit and have a hermit's life and that's it. The doctor told her a while ago that she was getting better and that perhaps she could go back to work pretty soon but she said that Margaret wants to buy a caravan and live on a beach, beach-combing all on her own, or get a flat and be a char woman. I told Margaret we are all very worried about her and that you would come out here if she thought it would do any good, but she just said she is all right and doesn't want to get better and is right enough on her own.

I can assure you that all Pauline has said about Margaret is true — she just has no will to do anything, and has virtually no feelings for anyone else — as she said to me. 'You know there are thousands of mental people in the world, well I am one of them so you'll have to get used to it.' Mary and I had quite a good talk with Doctor Bell, who thinks there is nothing we can do yet but be patient. She assures us that in time all will be well, but that Margaret is rather difficult to get through to and will not talk about things. Mum I don't think you should mention religion or chapel. Doctor says it seems to upset her.

I think all we can do is to wait and be patient. I know I couldn't be as patient as the Hospital staff is with her. When you ask her things, or try to put things to her she just shrugs and says she doesn't know, and it makes me feel like shaking her up, but I doubt whether it would do any good.

The doctor said that she had heard from you both, which was quite good as she can form a picture of Margaret's background together with our interview where she asked about Margaret's childhood and about the family in general as 'an outsider'.

Well don't worry you are now up to date and know the whole story; there is nothing we can do.

Pauline wrote on May 14:

Matron at Chelsea has asked me to reply to your letter because she is on holiday in Tasmania. Also because Dr Bell, (Margaret's doctor) asked me to go and see her last Thursday. I was wondering what she would want me for, but soon realised what a nice person she is. She wanted me to fill in a bit of Margaret's background, because you can realise just how difficult it is for her, not having anyone near to refer to. Anyway she said I had helped a lot, but I came out of her office feeling I had done very little. She said Margaret is much better now, not 100 percent, it will be a good while, but she does feel that she will be OK in time. She feels Margaret should go back to work, but Margaret does not want to do nursing any more. She seems to think that all work is futile, but really it is her outlook on life that is futile.

Margaret herself feels she would like a room in Melbourne and do odd jobs, but I can tell you she may find that difficult. Doctor knows this and is not at all keen for Margaret to do it.

I do feel that if Margaret would go back to Chelsea she could be out of Malvern Clinic next week. I may have to see doctor again next week, I will let you know.

Before posting my letter, I have just returned from seeing Margaret this evening, and she seems a lot brighter. I got to the hospital about 7pm and she was just going to have a bath, so she missed out on that and we talked for a while. Dr Bell has seen her, and Doctor Webb may see her tomorrow.

You would be amazed at the amount of young people here. I have never had much to do with this sort of thing before, so I start to wonder what is the matter with them all. I hope this letter helps a little.

Margaret, after the shock treatment cannot remember how she was before she went to Malvern. She was so depressed, used to cry a lot, but tonight she seemed really good, the best I have seen her since she came to the clinic.

I was still having regular letters of my own passing between Mum and Dad. With reports of my slow recovery, Mum got very concerned, quite naturally of course, but I was horrified when she wrote about coming out to Australia to be with me. I went into a deep depression: I was even suicidal: I had no wish to live: I could see no purpose in life. Discussions with Dr Bell became more difficult because I thought she might agree that my mother should visit me. In fact I don't think that was the case, but I was not to know at the time. So I signed for more ECT therapy, not particularly worried about the outcome which, as I write this, I shudder to think of, and now realise just how lucky I was to be in such a caring environment.

On May 29, Dr Bell wrote:

Dear Mrs Hockney,

My apologies for not having replied to your letter earlier. Margaret after showing some improvement as a result of the electrical treatment has again become depressed and it has been necessary to recommence the treatment. She is still an In Patient at the clinic and will be for some weeks yet.

It is unfortunate that in some cases of depression the illness tends to be prolonged but the eventual outlook is still good and in time Margaret should recover completely. I doubt if her coming to Australia had anything to do with precipitating her illness. Often there is no obvious cause and the breakdown would have occurred no matter where she was.

I had another four sessions of ECT under the same anesthetic at fortnightly intervals. Although the treatment certainly helped, I was far too comfortable with the routines of the clinic and made no effort to find a job and be discharged. Then came the real shock treatment. Dr Bell called me to say that I had been too long at Malvern Clinic. She was hoping that by now I would have been back at work. She asked me to agree to move out and be a voluntary patient at Larundel Hospital, a much larger institution than Malvern. There was not much choice, so I signed the relevant form and was taken to my new abode.

Larundel was awful, but I wrote home saying that it was fine. Everywhere was locked, rooms were opened one at a time. I slept in a twelve-bed dormitory. Screaming and moaning went on both day and night. Most residents were older, although I did manage to make friends with two of them. We still did Occupational therapy, but it was quite different. More like working in a factory, all doing the same thing. Food was not so nice and we were constantly supervised whilst using cutlery to eat. Bathing was also supervised. The only freedom was a walk within the locked grounds with any visitors who came.

It worked wonders for my complacency. I asked the doctor whether I could be discharged if I found a job. Yes, I could, but I don't think he expected me to find one very quickly. I got permission to visit the Nursing Commission in Melbourne to ask about vacancies. From there I got an interview for a midwife post at Mordialloc Hospital. What joy, I thought, Mordialloc was on the same line and just a few railway stations away from Chelsea.

I went for the interview; but by the time I finished explaining about my breakdown I was in tears. Although trying to sound confident and ready to work, my inside was shaking with uncertainty. My main reference was from Matron at Chelsea. Whilst I sat in that interview room with Matron at Mordialloc, she phoned Chelsea to ask for further recommendations on my abilities to be a midwife. She put the phone

down and offered me a job on a month's trial. Oh, fantastic. I would
have to be sure and get positive to make this work. Back at Larundel,
I got permission to get my scooter from Malvern, and within two
weeks I was working once more as a midwife. Only Matron knew my
history, so my new colleagues accepted me as perfectly normal. The
month's trial zoomed by. I became officially employed for as long as I
wished to stay. It was a busy little place and I enjoyed working there. I
made friends with colleagues, especially those who lived in the
attached nurses' home.

I needed a new philosophy or religion for life, so I booked into a
series of lectures in Melbourne on *The Nature and Destiny of Man*. Self-
help books were not abundant in those days, but I did read: *The Power
of Positive Thinking*, by Norman Vincent Peale; *How the Great Religions
Began*, by Joseph Gaer; as well as books about Jung, Freud and Adler's
theories of psychology. I had always enjoyed poetry and bought the
Oxford Book of English Verse and the volumes of comic, humorous and
metaphysical verse. It was a new road of self-discovery, finding out why
I was like I was. I wrote little poems of my own that released a bit of
creative energy and my own questioning of life. One was a longish
poem about loving your neighbour as yourself; the most important
lines I wrote were probably:

> *To love thy neighbour as thyself*
> *There must be self-love first.*
> *But surely that is selfishness,*
> *Of human faults the worst.*

This was in contrast to that old chorus of Jesus First, Yourself last
and Others in between, that I had been taught from childhood. I had
desperately tried to find Jesus, using hymns as poems, such as:

> *Master speak thy servant heareth*
> *Waiting for they gracious word*
> *Longing for the voice that cheereth*
> *Master let it now be heard.*
> *I am listening Lord for thee*
> *What hast thou to say to me*

I never did hear the Word. There was no response over many years
of searching.

Nevertheless life became more exciting, there was so much to explore in nature alone. I was never a big party-goer and fell asleep if I drank more than the odd glass of wine; but I did enjoy more of a social life and made the most of opportunity to travel around Australia and have fun instead of feeling the need to always be busy and working. Mind you, when I did work I had very high standards and kept up-to-date by reading professional magazines and research papers on all aspects of health and disease.

When I was discharged from Larundel I was not on any medication and to this day, nearly sixty years later, I have never had a relapse or re-admission to a clinic. Nor have I suffered depression. I have always had lots of energy, and a tendency to anxiety, especially concerning my Mother, but nothing that ever led me to a doctor or needed treatment.

7 Mum and Dad at Home

John was still at home with Mum and Dad. Mum's diaries give insight to the happenings between 1961 and 1962 and the family's concerns about me.

21 May 1961: *I asked David to go to Chapel but he said No. We chatted about worship and beliefs. David said some find it hard to believe in the supernatural and whereas there is so much beauty and good in the world, there is still much wickedness, and altho it is 1961 — men still do not love and help their neighbours. Our conversation was broken off, but I assume David has not accepted for himself the atonement and the Holy Spirit. He has high ideals and I have a very deep love for him — I shall think of him as my Abou Ben Adhem, and may God bless him.*

26 July 1961: *Philip rang up. They are accepted for Australia and will be given three weeks' notice. I can't help feeling upset and have a weep on my own. I'm sure they will be all right.*

15 September 1961: *David met us at Kings Cross station. He has bleached his hair and I did not at first recognise him. Took snaps of Philip, Mary and Beverley on deck, now a new era begins minus another, or three other members of our family.*

9 December 1961: *Arrived home from a day with Mrs Kirkby* (Pauline's mother) *7.30 pm, what a sight met me. A huge bouquet of flowers in a bowl on the table — just gorgeous! Evidently they had been left next door for me, and Kenneth brought them in when he got home. I tore open the accompanying envelope — From Margaret, through Interflora. I just sat down and gazed at them — overwhelmed with joy at the love these flowers have brought. Oh Margaret — thank you and God bless you, they are lovely.* (Mum's birthday was 10 December)

17 January 1962: *Margaret's Christmas parcel arrived at last. She has knitted me a lovely cardigan. Dad busy with his anti-smoking and cancer posters and letter writing. Listened into discussion on Peace and Nuclear disarmament between David and Dad. They don't always agree on their peace ideas.*

20 January 1962: *At last a letter from Margaret. She has seen doctor who says her complaint is nervous agitation — tho she feels well, — can*

Collins
One Day
Royal
Diary
1962

NUMBER 53

Arranged to meet David for coffee
at Collinsons at 11.30 am when I left
him in bed to go shopping — looked
around for a coat but saw nothing
to suit me — decided I'll have a
mac instead.   David did
not turn up for coffee - so I came
home — he rang up later to say he
got into Bradford later & met a friend
I was disappointed in him - but maybe
he forgot. —   He was home early
& we had dinner about 4-30 pm
Hens cold is soon gone.
Had a letter from Philip (or Mary
her writing) they seem to have
had a good Christmas & enjoyed
Margaret's visit.

Kenneth also had some letters
supporting his 'Smoking & Cancer'
posters.

Returned libraries — had 3ᵈ fine
on each

neither sleep not eat. She has been given tablets, which I hope will help her.

29 January 1962: *John gave me a pound this morning. As I made breakfast I said he never should have taken an expensive holiday if he had not saved for it. I only had coppers left and was tired of him and Dad never having any money. He said he didn't see why Dad hadn't, but I told him he was heading the same way but he would take no notice of me. There was still no letter from David or Margaret.*

1 February 1962: *Another letter from Margaret. Both Ken and I feel upset, but say little — she is in hospital with nerves and already is sleeping and eating — result of treatment since last week. Philip Mary and Bev have been to see her. I wrote to matron at Chelsea and hope we soon hear from Philip.*

9 February 1962: *No news from Margaret. Dad brought his pictures and has been painting them in the kitchen. We are almost silent — the atmosphere is awful, no reason really — but I feel so sick and can't help wondering about Margaret, but cannot confide in Ken, he is hard and unfeeling. Cried myself to sleep — John passing wanted to know what was wrong, but I just told him I'd be OK. Of course I shall, but had relieved pent up feelings.*

24 February 1962: *Started letter to Dr Webb, when Ken came in and looked over and asked who the letter was to. I felt the atmosphere broken so had to stop. Made Ken's breakfast and asked him to invite confidence not demand it. I have read and re-read my letter and do hope it reads to Dr Webb as I hope it should. I said how grateful we are to everyone concerned.*

27 February 1962: *Ken was annoyed this morning when, on asking me if I had sent the letter to Dr Webb — I said 'yes'. He says Dr may suggest Margaret goes to chapel, and that he, Ken is more concerned with her health physically than going to chapel! What next I wonder! Seems he does not want to face facts. I'm sorry we can't see this together — but feel sure I have done the right thing. He just has not read my letter with understanding, only with a critical mind. As I put the milk bottles out*

The back garden at Hutton Terrace that produced so much food for our Sunday tea.

— I saw plainly a cross in the snow. Funny, for no reason at all, a place where snow had parted in the shape of a cross — strange. I pondered.

23 March 1962: Ken announced he is going to Aldermaston at Easter to march. Doesn't ask if I mind or care what I do — says I can look after myself. Disarmament is more important. I too think it is a vital point and if he cared about his home too, I should encourage him more.

26 March 1962: Paul called tonight — told us David was on BBC TV last night on 'Monitor' and we did not have TV on! David ought to have let us know.

29 March 1962: Kenneth had a young couple on business, who are members of C.N.D. They have been married about five years, a German girl but very nice with Socialistic views. We had a pleasant evening, tho I maybe revealed some disapproval of the time he spends. They were amazed at his energies and non-stop posters and letters etc, but rather amused too. I guess that is looking at it from an outsider's point of view — inside — I'm sick and only by the Grace of God keep sane. I was upset and sleepless — Ken burned the night oil until 1.30 am.

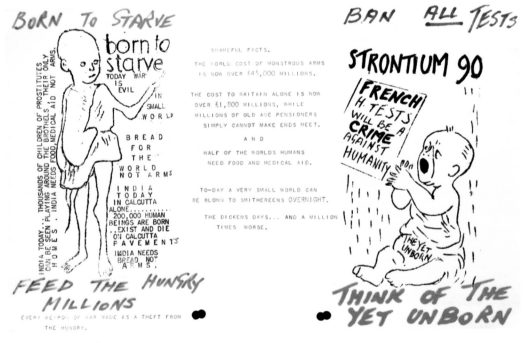

Dad's propaganda as art.

13 April 1962: *Trudy — a member of C.N.D. came to bring Kenneth more poster work. She can talk and talk — and we got from one thing to another. She is a Communist — she says Ken is too and I asked her to explain. She thinks — and says that many others do too, that Ken is wonderful and must spend all his money as she does on C.N.D. I agree, but she is single and lives alone, no other responsibilities. I make supper, which Trudy enjoys. Sorry I do not feel as they do — but they have no faith, at least Trudy admits it — but Ken says he Believes — it is all so puzzling to me — that they must see just the wrong things in life — true they must be faced, but we ought to see lovely things too — not dwell on evil and become morbid. My nerves are all on edge and they just talk and talk.*

24 April 1962: *David arrived — he looks well, but I'm not keen on his blond hair — it is nice to have him home. I think he will do very well when he leaves college in July, already has made quite a name for himself. He is to make a three-year contract with a London Art dealer who will pay him a monthly salary, but who also will have first preference to buy his pictures. He hopes to have a one-man exhibition at Geneva, Switzerland in six months' time. After another cup of tea together, David left for London about 4.45 pm taking a few 'home made' bakes.*

12 May 1962: *A letter from Philip this morning, but addressed to 'Master John', so I waited all day to see his letter. However John's letters are PRIVATE — so when I asked to see it, he refused. Just gave me items of news. Went to bed somewhat disappointed.*

26 May 1962: *John went to Dr High about his sore throat. John says Dr High says we mustn't take much notice of what Margaret says at present. It will be a long job. He and Dad had words about it — which is just torment to me.*

11 June 1962: *Ken decided to walk to Peel Park with me, but was not a pleasant walk. Someone enquired about Margaret, which set him off with all the complaints he could think of about my attitude to Margaret. If people enquire of me- he said, 'I tell them she is alright'. Poor man, he just won't accept sickness. I wonder if he will ever be ill himself.*

23 June 1962: *There always seems to be trouble at work where John is. Now he says he may stay at Rhona's (current girl-friend) for the night. I mustn't let my spirits down, but how I wish I could understand. Lord*

help me. Margaret ill in Australia. Philip and Mary — no letter over two weeks, Kenneth in Scotland Banning the bomb, David in London — no letter, Paul and Jean busy at home which is open to me at any time, but I must not impose on them. Lonely? Not in one way, but hurt, sick at heart and just don't understand. I'm alone, but not free. For more than thirty years I've struggled for peace in the home and everywhere — but I seem worse off than ever — only through all my mistakes and with the turmoil around me — even so — yes I believe in my heart there is peace even if I've tried and failed. Lord help me to trust you.

30 June 1962: *Letter from Philip all about Margaret. Ken says Philip has no right to write like that — yet it is true and I wanted facts. Kenneth does not seem able to accept that Margaret is ill in mind, and can only say how clever she is, how sincere, and that others have not done right by her and the doctor is giving her too much treatment etc. Ken goes to work — I am left on my own and think and think! Decide to probe! Rang up Dr Eddleston a psychiatrist whom Margaret saw at child guidance clinic from Belle Vue school and who is still practising. Also found Miss Copeland's address — matron of St Luke's Hospital and decided to get in touch with her. Went to bed and puzzled out Margaret's life from the beginning.*

6 July 1962: *I kept my appointment with Dr Eddleston at 11 am. He was very nice — proved to be the doctor who came to see me in an emergency after Paul was born and saved an abscessed breast. He has looked up reports — Margaret evidently visited him during 1951 for about a year. She was timid and reserved and hard to get through, but went regularly — was clever at school and did not like missing her biology lessons. Slow to make friends but loyal. He did not think she should have gone to Australia — not the type to mix — could have felt lonely — would be better to come home, or live near Philip — also to ask Dr Bell to send him report — when he may be able to help or suggest whether Margaret would be best at home, or to stay. He does not think the drugs do any good. Better he thinks — and I do too, to leave them alone and try to live normal again, unless it is a case of schizophrenia.*

David rang up this evening to tell us he is being given a gold medal and has a first class honours. He is so unconcerned, but it is a wonderful honour and he has evidently been pressurised to attend the ceremony, which previously he had no intention of doing. We are very proud of him and would like to go to London to see the ceremony and share the honours. I'm so glad David is still humble — but he has earned the prize. His only love is to paint? So far.

8 July 1962: Reply from Miss Copeland:

Dear Mrs Hockney, I was so distressed to see your letter and am so sorry to learn that Margaret has had a mental breakdown. I really cannot understand this for to me she did not have the temperament that would lead to such an occurrence. On no occasion do I remember her being at all mentally disturbed, she always seemed so placid. As far as I can remember she was thoroughly happy while at St Luke's — there was a nice relationship with the ward sisters, there was never any unhappiness as far as I was concerned, and she had many friends among the nurses. There was no occasion on which she came to my office with any cause of unhappiness, in fact she stands out in my memory as a nurse who worked well, studied well and had a good relationship with everybody, As with you I am at a loss to know how best I can help. Your consolation is that she has a good friend in Pauline Kirkby.

9 July 1962: *No letter from David, but he rang at 8.30 pm. He is still busy — but will see us on Friday. Graduation ceremony is at 11.30 am. I rang Cambria House (Salvation Army hotel at Kings Cross) and fixed up for Thursday night and the weekend. David said he has had a very happy birthday.*

12 July 1962: *Long night bus ride last night, and spent the morning around London waiting to sign in to Cambria House at 2 pm. Very tired and glad to go to bed early — but Kenneth no! He went out again with letters and some of his posters, which he had managed to smuggle in a carrier at the last minute — to the American Embassy.*

13 July 1962: *Was dismayed to find that Kenneth was locked out last night and had caused much commotion to get in. I felt very ashamed of him. The tickets that David said he would post had not arrived for the Convocation, so we set off early and were able to get duplicate ones. I enjoyed the short service very much and was glad for all those who had achieved an ambition. David looked fine in his gold lame jacket and gold-banded black gown and cap — his gold hair to match. The principal in his speech said that under David's eccentricities his heart was in his work and that not only was he to be honoured by the college, but would he*

thought, be one day an honour to his country. I'm glad that David is humble enough not to care too much about presentations but realises that his work alone will get him a place in the world.

22 July 1962 (David had been home a few days): *David arrived down at 11 am for breakfast. I sat by the stove and wrote up my diary — occasionally chatting with David. Ken rather fussy and David resents it. I got a word in about the day we went to College — how we felt not very welcome, partly understood — but I thought that without a fuss, David could have seemed glad we were there. I guess he was all het up himself and anyhow we enjoyed his company later.*

1 August 1962: *No post again — only for Kenneth who has advertised his 'Hiroshima photographs' and got several orders.*

Those children and people who suffered from the 'fall out' look dreadful and we certainly should hope there will be no more — but Oh! To see these pictures all over the house — in the bedroom when I wake up, in the bathroom basin as he develops them, in the front room drying out, it makes me sick! Morning, noon and night — on display. Ken was up and down stairs until 2.30 am, cellar to attic constantly with his buckets of water and photographs.

THE FACE OF HIROSHIMA

JAPAN— ONE ATOM BOMB KILLED OVER 80,000 HUMANS— ONE HYDROGEN BOMB EQUALS 750 ATOM B MEMBER JAPAN — ONE ATOM BOMB — ONE CITY DIE

Dad is deeply concerned.

15 September 1962: *Great news this morning — Margaret writes to say she started work last Monday — wrote Tuesday so had just worked one day. Oh thank God and I do hope and pray she may continue to work and be happy and live and love a full and useful life. A year ago today we saw the 'Fairsky' sail away with Philip, Mary and Beverley. So much has happened since then — good things and sad ones. They have given us both joy and great anxiety — let us hope it is over now and things run smoother for them all. David rang this morning to say he will not be coming until next week. It was nice to hear him — sorry we must wait another*

week but glad he let me know. I get so worked up inside with longings when I hear of or from any of them, but I don't think I look worked up. I'm glad it doesn't show what I feel. Bless 'em all.

16 September 1962: *(Ken has a C.N.D. Visitor Mr Knowles) supper brought more talk. I felt so tired; he and Ken are both full of complaints about bombs and politics etc. He told me that Ken told him and two others in a train going to the march in Blackpool that I was the best wife anyone could have. I ask you? Could it be true?*

12 December 1962: *Letter from Philip said Margaret visited last week and she is much better, back to her normal self again.*

8 Under the Shadow of the Red Rock

Peggy, a midwife colleague at Mordialloc lived in the nurses' home. She had a Volkswagen Beetle and wanted a co-driver to travel to Central Australia. It sounded exciting and I was keen but had not saved much cash in the first six months of working again. I felt really fit, so I signed on with a private nursing agency to work during my off-duty from Mordialloc. This was an accepted regime at the time. Work hard and then enjoy touring Australia. So for the next two months I ate, slept and worked.

Agency work was different from what I had so far experienced. It could be sitting all night with an elderly gentleman to make sure his pacemaker was working — just a case of checking his pulse every hour and being aware of the signs of failing pacemakers. Some nights were at the Freemasons Hospital, on a male genito-urinary ward, where I was doing post-operative bladder washouts in a very posh hospital. I also worked in private nursing homes. There was one quite busy maternity hospital, which also had five geriatric patients: three women in one room and two men in another. I often went to a home that had eight elderly patients and sixteen mentally-handicapped babies and children. The children were admitted to give their parents respite. Originally Matron had only taken four at a time, but over the years some parents had abandoned their children and so gradually the numbers and ages had increased. Although Matron knew where most of the parents were she never insisted that they should retrieve their child. The handicaps were severe: hydrocephaly, microcephaly and varying degrees of spasticity. Many children had sleepless nights emitting periodic screams, which caused the old people to have fitful nights. Matron tried hard in caring for the children, who could hardly have been a financial asset to her. There was a specially-employed day staff to dress the children and take them for walks outside in prams or wheelchairs. Matron would also take some of the children out with her when she and her husband had car trips.

Beetling to the Red Rock in 1963.

After two months of this full-time work, I took my paid leave at Mordialloc and had a small leaving party. Matron very kindly assured me that if I wanted to return, I would be welcome. That was a real confidence boost. I realised how fortunate I had been to be back in full-employment. Mum's letters were not bothering me, so that was another bonus.

Peggy and I set off on our three-week holiday. Nothing was booked but we hoped to reach Alice Springs and Ayers Rock (Uluru). To reach the car train at Port Augusta in South Australia took us three days. Our car was loaded with camping gear; we had hired a tent and camp beds and carried gallon cans of water and a can of petrol. We bought a sack of fresh oranges just before crossing the border from Victoria to South Australia but were not allowed to take them over the border because of the risk of spreading fruit-fly. So we bought an orange squeezer and replaced the water in one of the gallon containers with orange juice. We never drank much of the juice, as water was more refreshing. The next day the orange juice leaked, exuding a sticky smelly mess in the sweltering heat of the car. That taught us about border control and fruit-fly risks. We wouldn't do that again.

Once we had driven the car on to the freight truck we explored our surroundings. It was an amazing train. We had a two-berth cabin for the two-night trip; there were carriages for eating, game playing, chatting with other passengers and just sitting to watch the view as the train chugged to the station at Alice Springs. We drove the car off the train and looked around to find a camping ground for the night. As the weather was scorching hot, we decided to sleep under the stars without the tent. I woke in the middle of the night — frozen. I couldn't see Peggy so I carted my blanket into the wash-house and settled down to sleep in a bath. Some startled campers making an early get-away rudely awakened me a few hours later.

There was a glorious sunrise and I felt excited by the isolation of Alice Springs. It was smaller than I expected. Three pubs attracted the leisure seekers, but unmissable was Dr Flynn's grave and monument which marks the spot over which John Flynn's ashes were cast from an aeroplane flying over Mount Gillen, which towers behind it. We saw the Flying Doctor Headquarters that Flynn had pioneered. There was a tourist shop and memorial gardens to Aboriginal artist Albert Namatjira, who had a wonderful peaceful philosophy. He lived a simple life, sharing the wealth from his successful picture sales with his fellow

Aborigines according to their law of kinship. Because of his fame as an artist he was the first Aborigine granted Australian citizenship in 1957; as well as being eligible to vote, he could buy alcohol. His kinship friends shared the alcohol but he was accused of breaking the white man's law by supplying alcohol to Aborigines. This saddened him and he lost the will to paint. He died a few years before we were there, but his paintings of the nearby landscape live on.

The sand in Alice Springs was dry and red although we were told that when the rains came, it was as though a green carpet of vegetation was laid over all the ground. The next day we planned to drive to Ayers Rock, about three hundred miles away. We had been warned to arrive before sunset otherwise getting lost in the dark was a possibility. June, a winter in Australia, was ending; but day-time was still very hot. Sunrise was just after 7 am. The sun would set at about 6 pm. So we had nearly eleven hours of daylight. Away we went at 7 am armed with notes about the route and where to get fuel; the car stocked with emergency petrol and our gallon of water. We intended to have a lunch-break at Mount Ebenezer.

We had never seen such roads, sort of red sand-tracks interspersed with sand rocks, creeks, gum trees and occasional sightings of Aboriginal families with their camels, dogs and possessions, all on walkabout to a new place to live. Usually they were a good distance from the road, but occasionally we would see them nearer to us. After about sixty miles, a horse appeared seemingly from nowhere and ran in front of the car.

He must have kicked up some rock, because our windscreen was shattered. We bagged the broken glass and proceeded, but soon realised that warm windy sand blowing through the windscreen would no doubt blind us before we got much further. So we decided to go back to Alice and find a garage. Unbelievably, fate lent a hand. A truck pulled up behind us with three young Australians who were prepared for such an incident.

They actually had heavyweight plastic with them, plus scissors and tape to attach it; but they also warned us not to drive to Ayers Rock with this temporary screen. There would be no garage there. They directed us where to go for help and so back we drove to Alice Springs. We were lucky again, VW Beetles were a popular car and the garage fitted a new windscreen.

Thanks mate. Me in the middle of Australian helpers.

The horse with no name that kicked a stone through our windscreen

After another night in the Alice camp, we were on the road again. It was frightening, exciting, spectacular and humbling. There would be strange names on signposts, curves in the sand road, more tribes and animals and the occasional petrol station. The sun illuminated changing colours of the entire landscape which was mountainous, yet we drove on level ground. There were gum trees with hawks searching for prey on the sunburnt earth, occasional cattle stations and homesteads. Sadly, we saw cows that had died through heat and dehydration. I wondered who was a true Australian in this so-varied land. This was nothing like Melbourne or Sydney. Aborigines looked a dusty-grey colour. The children had wild black hair and little or no clothing.

They mingled with the dogs and other animals. The whole trip would warrant a book of its own, but all I have are scattered memories of a raw and wonderful nature, offering breathless surprises and coloured chasms. We drove on with little need of trivial conversation, swapping the driver's seat occasionally in that little sand-coloured Volkswagen Beetle: total harmony.

We gave them an apple. How can he hide it with no clothes on?

Under the shadow of this red rock. Camping at Ayers Rock 1963.

We realised the sun was getting lower. There were sand hills in our path that made us deviate a bit; keeping in the right direction was a worry. Gradually, in the far distance, we saw the shape that we were heading for. We felt so safe to know we were nearly there. Just in time before that gigantic sun disappeared from the horizon we saw the sign Ayers Rock, and drove under it to the rock itself. We had been driving the full eleven hours of daylight. We were delighted to be welcomed by a small group of campers and invited to share their meal. With our tent pitched and camp-beds ready, we joined our fellow tourists. They related their experiences and suggested what to see.

The natives called the rock Uluru long before it was called Ayers Rock, a large solid sandstone monolith, dome-shaped, covering an area of twelve hundred acres and rising more than eleven hundred feet above the surrounding plateau. Ayers Rock was a sacred mythical rock to the local Aboriginal tribes and a place of awe to tourists.

White tourists had named markings crudely such as Kangaroo's Tail, Napoleon's Hat, Wine glass, the Stairs. At least the names helped us identify where we were as we travelled around the red marvel. The first day Peggy and I simply walked around the entire rock, over five miles in scorching heat. The rock was not just smooth, there were caves to enter and cave-paintings of animals and rituals. We saw the named landmarks, shady areas, and parts glistening in the bright sun. There were bushes, grassy patches and steep cliff faces.

There was no marked trail to climb and no guiding rope for the start of the climb. A rope was installed a year later in 1964. Some people said tourists should not climb Ayers Rock at all, because it was full of the souls of Aborigines and should be respected as their sacred place. Climbing the rock was still an individual choice. Peggy had a dream that she would be in danger if she climbed to the top. I was not sure, nor was I particularly athletic. When we reached the place to start the climb we both set off clinging to the rock holds, wearing no special clothing or shoes, merely dressed in shorts and tops for the heat of the day. There were maybe a dozen others above us. About seven hundred feet up we arrived at Bill Harney's Lookout, a famous landmark in memory of Bill Harney, a ranger. We rested and looked across at the Olga Mountains and the little pools of water with mountain flowers growing on the rock face. I felt stimulated and was ready to climb to the top but Peggy recalled her dream and went no further. She descended as I continued. A new experience for me, but I felt reassured by the sight of fellow climbers. The trail seemed to go on and on, upwards and further upwards, me clinging to the rock, scarcely daring to turn one way or another. After what seemed hours I arrived. I felt as though I had landed on another planet. There was a vast space.

The only way is down: self-portrait after climbing to top of Ayers Rock.

Walking was not easy because of the craters, pools, shrubs and clumps of flowers. The heat was quenched by quite a strong wind that surprised me. Normally several people would arrive together and take photos.

I took my own, setting the camera precariously on one rock whilst I clung to another and hoped the wind would not claim my camera. I managed a frightened looking self-portrait. The climb down was petrifying. All the people I had seen must have been going down, not up. I was all alone and the way down was a long, steep rock-face. Hymns of help came to mind as I sought for guidance from my great Jehovah to guide me through this foreign land: I was weak but He was mighty, please guide me with his powerful hand. Maybe God spoke because I arrived safely to the relief of Peggy. Mum would have been delighted, if I had told her.

We spent several days at the same camp, meeting new tourists and bidding farewell to others, sharing our evening meal. There would be no more than twelve at any one time, everyone in awe of this wonderful red centre of Australia. Our drive back to Alice Springs was another thrilling adventure. Now familiar with the territory and the passing nomads, we totally enjoyed the ride, reaching Alice less than an hour before sunset. The next day we drove to Stanley Chasm. We stood in amazement as the sunlight passed through the chasm reflecting the weathered minerals of the rocks into all variations of colour.

The freight carriage with cars on the train back to Port Augusta was derailed at a place called Finke — if memory serves — so we continued without the cars. We had to spend two nights in Port Augusta where we amused ourselves whilst waiting for them to arrive.

Our next target was Mildura, back into Victoria. We drove through the Barossa Valley, did some wine tasting and picnicked on the river Murray. We stopped at Mount Gambia to see the blue lake, famous for its cerulean colour. Our final camp-night was near Geelong, then back to Melbourne ready for work after an absolutely marvellous holiday. That little Beetle served us well.

Pauline was working in Christchurch, New Zealand, and I was keen to follow her there. I got a job as a midwife in Melbourne, working night-duty; on my nights off I worked for the agency again. I stored my scooter and cabin-trunk at Chelsea and soon earned enough to buy a flight to New Zealand. Letters from Mum were not upsetting me anymore. Conversely, my letters home became more interesting and informative.

9 Maoris and Hot Springs

Before going to New Zealand I applied for Nurse and Midwife registration. This involved sending signed photocopies of nursing registration certificates to the Nursing Commission of New Zealand. There was some delay with this so when I arrived in New Zealand I could not take a nursing post.

Pauline had an acquaintance working as a house-keeper and looking after two children at an Outward Bound school. She was told she could have a friend stay with her. So I went to stay as her friend. She met me at the nearest train station, Blenheim, forty miles away, drove back on the winding, unmade road, between mountains and beautiful bays and rivers, to the Outward Bound School at Anakiwa. It was a training-school for fifteen to seventeen-year-old boys offer-ing a tough course of obstacles, tracking, bridge-making and survival skills if

Me at Pendennis Maori Hostel 1963.

stranded in the bush. They killed their own meat or fish, learned which plants are edible and lit their own fires to cook their food. The course lasted six weeks and they aimed to get enough marks to merit a certifi-cate. Prince Philip had visited. The children at the house where I stayed were thrilled when he shook hands with them. I spent a week at the school then had a memorable trip to Picton on the mail boat. I met Pauline at Picton at the top of New Zealand's South Island and we boarded the ferry to go to Wellington on the North Island.

As my nurse registration was still not complete, I looked in the paper for a temporary job. There was an advert for a packer, no experience needed. It was for six weeks. I applied, got the job and had to start next day. I had not even arranged where to spend the night.

Pauline had found herself work as housekeeper to a gentleman near Lake Taupo, a trip north, so I said farewell to her then rang lots of hostels and finally booked in at Pendennis, a Maori hostel. I was the only Pakeha staying there amongst about twenty Maori girls. It was a short walk from the hostel to my new job. I was employed by an Australian chemist who travelled each year to Wellington, to make Eugene hair dye. My job was to pour the strong dyes into Winchester bottles, label them with the appropriate colour of dye, then cork them and pack into cartons, which I had to unflatten. The job was for six weeks because that was how long it had taken in previous years. As I worked alone, I soon discovered the quickest and cleanest method to work. I finished the job in three weeks instead of six, but got paid for the full six. The following year when I was back in England, I got a letter from the chemist asking if I would help her again.

I stayed at the Pendennis Maori hostel for four weeks, a joyful place where girls from the country were helped to settle and find work in Wellington. The cook invited me to the local Ngati Poneke club, where Maori girls would practise action songs and dancing, always ready to perform for visiting dignitaries. I was honoured to be given a grass skirt, and allowed to embroider a tapestry bodice and headband with the Ngati Poneke Club design. Whilst I was there, the Governor General's wife, Lady Ferguson, visited the hostel. The Maori girls did a display of Action song, and we were all introduced. When the Lady-in-Waiting, Miss Virginia Lucas, heard my name, she replied, 'Oh I know an English artist by the name of Hockney.' She was certainly surprised to know that he was my brother; I was equally surprised that she knew of him.

When I left Wellington I travelled by luxury land-liner to visit Pauline at Lake Taupo. Coffee and tea were served on the bus and there was a lunch-break at Mount Ruapehu, one of several non-active volcanoes that we passed on the route. With Pauline I visited hot springs and chemical pits at Waiotapu, an amazing area of natural phenomena, with opaque sheets of coloured steam smelling of sulphur. We marvelled at the pools of bubbling boiling mud. We went in a Maori Meeting House at Rotorua, a massive building where Maoris meet for special events. Some took blankets and slept there if they had travelled far. There were so many wonderful and historic places to visit.

Pauline had another housekeeping job in Gisborne, so we travelled the bumpy road by a bus that also delivered mail and newspapers. The driver just threw them out of the bus-window to the houses. The mail-bus took nine hours to travel the two hundred miles to Gisborne

on the East Coast of North Island. I stayed two nights. A neighbour of
the family Pauline started work with phoned up a hospital and got me
a job as a midwife — just like that. By now my registration was sorted
out, so next day I travelled by service car, which delivered mail and
newspapers same as the bus had done, to Te Puia Springs sixty miles
north of Gisborne.

Te Puia had a new and large hospital, even though it was only a small
town. It had been a cottage hospital since about 1900 and was rebuilt
in 1950, with an eighteen-bed maternity annexe added. The hot spring
was possibly the reason for the original hospital, as the water was
thought to be health-giving. When I arrived, there was a hot water
swimming bath, with water flowing directly from the hot spring; sometimes it would be too hot to even dip a foot into.

Nearly all the patients were Maori but spoke English as well as their
native language. As the hospital had an extensive catchment area,
pregnant women were often admitted when their babies were due.

They helped out in the wards and learnt care of the newborn. Usually they had their guitars, making lots of
music, singing and dancing.

On my first evening in the Nurses' home,
I introduced myself to the colleagues with
whom I would be living. Incredibly, two of
them trained at St Luke's and were from
Bradford. Pauline joined me at Te Puia
after her housekeeping job. She worked on
the General side of the hospital. I worked
on Maternity side.

The hospital secretary was from Hull

Action songs from patient and staff.

and three others were from Yorkshire. Jean
and Joan from St Luke's had an Austin A40
car and five of us shared driving to tour the North Island, booking
motels or camp-sites at each destination. We planned the route and I
sent a copy home with a map.

It was a fascinating holiday. We saw volcanos, fiords, history and
Maori culture. New Zealand had so much variety, yet it was not over-
crowded. During the holiday Pauline returned by boat to England. I
was not sure about returning home. I had been offered a job as a
Midwifery tutor, so was wondering about gaining more qualifications
to take that job.

White angels. Pauline and me at TePuia Springs Hospital.

Nov. 1963		Nights	Miles
29	Travel to Opotiki in the Bay of Plenty	1	200
30	To Rotorua	1	92
Dec.			
1	Up to Aukland	2	150
3	Travel via Kaikohe Forest to Paihia in the Bay of Islands	3	243
6	Down to Tekuiti	1	300
7	Visit Waitomo glow worm caves and travel to Mount Egmont	2	184
9	Visit Wanganui	1	90
10	Down to Wellington	2	
11	Wave Pauline off back to England sailing on North Star		
12	Up to Lake Taupo	1	248
13	To Napier	1	100
15	Return to Te Pauia ready for work on 16th		

The blue line roughly marks our route.

North Island holiday itinerary.

Back at TePuia, all the staff had an invitation to the wedding of a Maori couple that none of us knew. We were advised to attend because the more guests there were, the more happy years the marriage would have. The church was at Tokomaru Bay, where arum lilies grew wild and the whole place was idyllic. Lots of friends and relatives travelled from far and stayed in the local Maori Meeting House, where all the gifts were displayed. The reception was finger-food, the speciality being wild pig that had been slow-cooked in large holes dug out of the hot earth and covered with the dugout soil for several days. It was the most delicious and tender pork I have ever eaten. Instead of reception speeches, Maori dancing and singing entertained us. We ate at long trestle tables, loaded with food and drink. It was a happy and friendly day.

Now that Pauline was on her way back to England, Mum was putting on a lot more pressure wondering when I would be returning. Truth was that I could have happily stayed between New Zealand and Australia forever and maybe have taken the Midwife Tutor's course; but the pull from Mum was too strong. On reflection I can see how I was still cocooned by limitations of my mothers' beliefs. Work responsibilities did not worry me at all, in fact I loved my work and could easily adapt to any challenges. But away from work I was still not free from my mother. I was too mixed up emotionally to follow my dream of staying in Australia. I felt compelled to start finding a ship to return home. I planned one more holiday after leaving TePuia Hospital and then would go to see Philip, Mary and Beverley in Sydney.

I went with Joan and Jean on a South Island holiday. They were going to work in Timaru but drove me as far as Queenstown, where I got the plane to Te Anau to walk the Milford Track — known as the finest walk in the world.

I spent the night in Te Anau and next morning met my fellow trackers. Forty-two of us gathered to walk over a narrow bridge to the launch that would take us to our first night at Glade House. Most of us were enjoying the hot and sunny scenery on the deck until the boat caused so much spray that we were all soaked. We laughed at ourselves and got to know each other. We were a mixed group, young, old and many different nationalities. We all had our rucksacks of luggage, some lighter, others looked very heavy. Two packhorses carried supplies of food and emergency gear. I posted a letter to Mum at Te Anau, but had to warn her there would be no more post-boxes along our walking route.

On day one we had a ten-mile walk through forest and meadows to Pompolona. We slept in large dormitories full of cosy bunks. Food was excellent throughout. Day two started with a five mile walk upwards through thick bush land, rising nineteen hundred feet to the McKinnon Pass. Then we walked four miles down the other side to Quintin, a lovely spot

New Zealand South Island holiday.

surrounded by mountains and waterfalls where we spent two nights. We went to the Sutherland Falls, the highest waterfall in New Zealand. Standing underneath at the bottom for a different view of the cascade was fun. A thirteen-mile walk next day on level ground took us to the end of the track at Sand Fly Point. Whilst waiting for the launch to take us the last two miles to Milford, sand flies had a good meal of everyone with their blood sucking bites. It was a lovely few days; we were totally tuned-in to nature and peaceful companionship.

At the end
of the
Milford
Track.

It was a wonderful finale to my time in New Zealand.

Two days later, in mid-February 1964, I flew back to Melbourne and soon had another job on night duty at St Andrews Hospital. On nights off I worked again with the private agency. I was now saving-up for my fare back to England. I went to the travel agent and booked a cabin on the Himalaya, which was due to sail in October. I spent the last three months in New South Wales near Philip and Mary, working at a Repatriation Hospital for ex-servicemen at Turra Murra. It was very pleasant and there was a koala bear sanctuary nearby. A nice few months to end my stay Down Under.

We got news from Mum that Dad had been diagnosed with diabetes. He diagnosed himself in London because of his excessive thirst, and getting lost on the underground. He bought two booklets for him and Mum to read about it, and then got diabetes officially confirmed by blood tests at Bradford Royal Infirmary.

10 Bringing it All Back Home

I chose to travel back on the P&O's *Himalaya* partly because it was a one-class ship, but mostly because of the ports of call where I had day-tours. I would be stopping at Melbourne, Adelaide, Perth, Colombo, Bombay, Aden, Port Said, Piraeus, Marseilles, Gibraltar, and Tilbury in London. The ship sailed on October 15, 1964 and arrived in England on November 16.

The trip was marvellous, but returning to England was an anti-climax. There was a torrential rainstorm as we docked.

Pauline had driven her Morris Minor to Tilbury where she also met Mum and Dad. David was in Zurich but now had a London flat in Powis Terrace that he said we could use for the night. He sent a letter to Mum and Dad:

I hope you enjoy your stay and approve of my reorganisation of the flat. Without the fire in the living room it's a bit cold at the moment, but when it's all fixed up I think it should be very comfortable and stylish. I have nearly finished the lithographs I came here to do, and will leave here tomorrow for Paris and hope to be back in London next week. It's hard work in this lithography place. They start work at 7am so I'm obliged to be here and supervise the printing till 6 pm, — a little exhausting.

Has Margaret started back at St Luke's yet? I'm sure she couldn't face it again after exotic Australasia — or could she?

Pauline handed the driving to me. As I drove through London, Dad was feeling peckish and kept pointing out eating-places: 'Look there is Lyons corner house, they are good and cheap.' I kept driving, no point telling him about impossible parking at these London eateries. I drove to Liverpool Street station to collect my luggage that had been sent from the ship, seven baggages of it, mostly filled with gifts.

There was a present for everyone: koalas and boomerangs from Australia, tikis and translucent Paua shells from New Zealand; elephants from Colombo; silk fabric and carvings from Bombay; two stools that I won on a shore excursion in Arabia, one shaped as a camel, the other with storage space under the seat; an Ali Baba basket, plus the rug I made in the clinic. I had to fit all this into the little car and could scarcely see through the windows as I drove to King's Cross to send the lot by goods train to Bradford. Mum, Dad and Pauline went by tube to King's Cross, where we had a snack before heading for David's flat. The lights of London streets and shops were getting brighter after the gloomy grey of the post war 1950's. Dad insisted that we saw the Christmas lights in Oxford Street and Piccadilly Circus, which were well worth the visit before we wearily dropped into our beds.

A few days later, gifts distributed, the excitement was replaced with miserable November weather and me trying to decide where to work. I visited Pauline, who was district nursing in Bath, and went to see some shipmates in London. But job hunting was not so easy as abroad and I was a bit home-sick for the climate and life in Australia. My money was spent on the trip and the gifts, but my accountant brother Paul came to the rescue. He put me in touch with a private midwife in Harrogate who was working seven days a week alone and was desperately in need of a partner. After making enquiries about the job I joined her, working at the private hospital.

She lived in a large Victorian house. There was an empty flat above hers, which I rented and started right away sharing the work by doing twenty-four hour shifts in turn. Many of our patients were from the American air base at Menwith Hill. It was a five-minute walk to work from the flat in Wordsworth Crescent. Pauline left her job in Bath and joined me. We shared a bigger flat on the top floor. She got a job as a midwife in a local Maternity Unit. I bought a Moped and got a second job at a private nursing home in Leeds, a mother-and-baby home where unmarried pregnant girls could live and work for a couple of months before being delivered. Their babies were left for adoption. The 1960s was an era of stigma for unmarried

London's West End in the winter of 1964

pregnancies; leaving their babies behind must have been heart-wrenching for the girls. Strangely, there were three or four elderly patients to nurse in the same home.

Although Mum and Dad were now living alone, John, David and me kept visiting albeit for short sessions. We probably all found Mum a magnet and had to pull back from her powerful energy. I certainly did. Paul, Jean and their four children were a godsend; she adored baby sitting and watching them develop, and she could listen to Paul preaching in chapels. She would confide in Jean about frustrations with Dad.

According to Mum, we never stayed long enough. She would say we never had a proper chat or outing alone, or whatever she felt was missing. She wanted to be home for me, so she left a perfect little school-dinner job. I did not want to be home with her; neither did I want her to suffer on my account, so I kept smiling, trying to include her in my life. It was an impossible task. Sometimes my life seemed as though it would never be my own. Own? What a word. I was owned by my mother. How could I dispute that? I had witnessed birth, death, health, and disease; yet I remained imprisoned in my guilty world of trying to please mother.

Not just me. She always regretted David's return to his own home as well. Mum and Dad visited David in his flat near Notting Hill and Portobello Road as often as they could, especially for the CND march every Easter. David was usually, well should I say always busy, but he would book them seats at shows or suggest places to visit. Mum would clean and take washing to the newly-opened launderette nearby and leave his place spic and span. Even when David went away on trips to America or Europe, Mum and Dad would still use the flat. Sometimes they overlapped with friends to whom David had offered lodgings. The friends always had to give way to the parents.

Mum was a good and busy woman who could not understand why my father could not see her point of view. She went to night school to make hats, gloves and pattern drafting; she sewed clothes constantly and beautifully for all the family and others in need. Gardening was a joy to her, so were visits to lonely or shut-in people and poor families. An excellent cook, she coped with Dad's diabetic food, as well as any visitors whom she continued to welcome. Account books of income and spending were meticulously kept. The house was clean, although tidiness was difficult because Dad had cluttery hobbies. Mum thrived on people. When there was only Dad and her, he would be busy and she would be unhappy.

Dad had unlimited energy and could be up all hours to complete whatever he was doing. He painted large posters to carry on marches for Campaign for Nuclear Disarmament, the Peace Pledge Union or marches against The American war in Vietnam. He would frequently spend a couple of nights in cheap accommodation if the march was not in London. Some were day-trips to Blackpool or Scarborough when he would leave very early and return in the early hours next morning. He made posters for charities such as Oxfam, and associations for diabetes and arthritis, and for his own anti-smoking campaigns.

He painted pictures and submitted them for exhibition. Although that was not a very successful side of his hobbies the activity kept him busy and added a bit more clutter to the house. Always keen on photography he had a dark-room in the back attic now that the boys no longer needed bedrooms up there. Mum insisted on keeping the front attic as a guest bedroom for when David or John visited. My old bedroom remained for me, although it now doubled up as a sewing room.

Mum didn't like Dad using water from the bathroom for his photography as it made a mess, so he would carry a bucket up from the cellar to the attic to pour into his developing tank and printing dishes. Wouldn't he have loved digital cameras!

The photos he was most keen to take were neither landscapes nor portraits, although he would include those now and again at weddings or group outings. Most of the time he had a tripod set up in front of the television with his shutter release cable attached to the camera, and maybe a little title sign on top of the television with the date and event. Some of his topics were man's first step on the moon, horrors of war, Vietnamese children, documentaries and as time went on, anything about David and his pictures. Dad had to be there promptly in time for each programme. There were no videos or repeats. He triggered the shots then he would develop and print. Some of the war victims would have many copies printed. He incorporated them into the posters for his marches.

Another compulsion was letter-writing, and he had his own campaign against smoking. He would reverse Hockney to Yenkcoh or call himself Kenlaw if he wanted to hide his identity. Sometimes there would be acknowledgements, sometimes not. He wrote to Izal, the

One of Dad's Ban the Bomb posters

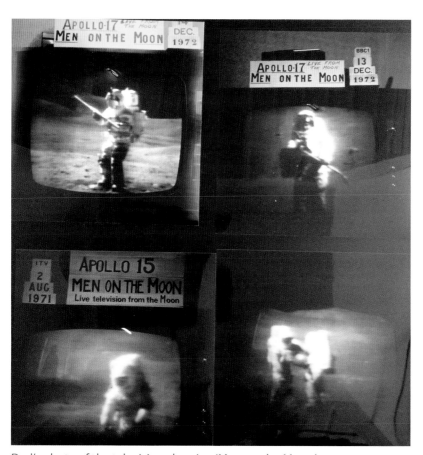

Dad's photo of the television showing 'Men on the Moon'

germicide toilet-paper company, to congratulate them on the quality of the perforations between sheets. It kept him very busy and I thought what he was doing was fascinating. He was not a good speller, had left school aged fourteen, but he had strong convictions and let them be known.

His photos were sometimes a bit blurry, possibly caused by his failing eyesight.

John had been corresponding with Philip and was keen to join him in Australia. He rented a furnished cottage in Bingley for two pounds a week to start married life with Alwyn. The wedding was on April 3, but the day didn't go too well. Mum and Dad were nearly forgotten to be chauffeured so were late arriving. The wedding buffet was late and the food looked meagre in the large room. John had many friends and a good sense of humour so the memory is of a happy day. Pauline lent them her car for their honeymoon as John's had broken down. Hoping for a change of fortune, John and his wife were waved-off at London airport as they emigrated to Sydney, Australia on July 12, 1965.

Just before Christmas that year, Dad had his first hospital admission. He had been eating more food than Mum had cooked for him. She was trying to help him keep to his diet, but on this night he ate an extra two tins of beans and was sick. By morning he was very dopey. He insisted on going to work, but was sent home at 11am for dozing-off. Mum phoned the doctor who advised her what to do, but sickness and doziness continued. Dad kept saying he would soon be fine. When the doctor said he could not be responsible for the outcome if Dad didn't go to hospital he still objected, even though he could hardly talk. Eventually, semi-comatose, he agreed and the ambulance took him to Bradford Royal Infirmary, where he soon had an intravenous drip in place and constant nursing and medical care. He grumbled about being there, both to staff and visitors. We all saw him on Christmas Day looking much better but still refusing the prescribed daily insulin injections, saying he would take the tablets more regularly. On January 7, 1966, Dad decided to go home. He signed himself out against medical advice. He said he was too busy to stay in hospital. As soon as he got home he started with meetings, going into town shopping and doing his posters and photos. He was admitted in another coma a month later. That time he agreed to start injecting insulin. Within a couple of days he proudly stated that he could give himself the injections.

THE EDITOR,
TELEGRAPH & ARGUS,
HALL INGS,
BRADFORD 1.

18 HUTTON TERRACE,
BRADFORD 2.

29TH. OCTOBER 1968

KHS-1
16

Sent to T&A.

DEAR SIR,

I WISH TO POINT OUT THAT THE REPORT OF MY
DISPLAYING AN ANTI-SMOKING POSTER ON SATURDAY OUTSIDE
THE BRADFORD COOPERATIVE SOCIETY IN SUNBRIDGE ROAD WAS
PROMINENTLY WORDED AS FOLLOWS :(AND TAKEN FROM A RECENT
PRESS REPORT) OF WHICH A COPY IS ENCLOSED.

CIGARETTES KILL 300,000 PEOPLE
A YEAR.

ALSO ADDED.

CIGS KILL SEVEN TIMES MORE PEOPLE
THAN ROAD ACCIDENTS. — *DOCTOR*

SURELY THE ABOVE FACTS ARE VERY DISTURBING , AND
THE SUPERMARKETS ARE VERY GUILTY IN PRESSING THE SALE OF
CHEAP CIGARETTES , HAVING POSTERS FOR SAME DISPLAYED
PROMINENTLY IN THEIR WINDOWS, *while knowing the persistent*
warnings of on the danger of smoking Cigarettes made by the
Royal College of Physicians I THINK ALL CIGARETTE MANUFACTURERS SHOULD BE
COMPELLED TO STATE A WARNING ON THE CIGARETTE PACKETS RE
EXCESSIVE SMOKING OF CIGARETTES.

WILL YOU PLEASE PUBLISH THE ABOVE FACTS.

YOURS FAITHFULLY,

KENNETH HOCKNEY.

They Poster was NOT simply
worded Cigarettes Kill but
recent) Cigarettes KILL 300 000 people a year
s Report)

This is much more important

'Killer' badges for children

Cigarette warning

Yorkshire Post Reporter

SCHOOLCHILDREN may soon be wearing badges proclaiming " Smoking is harmful. Safeguard your health." round a drawing of a black spot on a lung.

Because of his dissatisfaction in the campaign of the National Society of Non-Smokers, Mr. Kenneth Hockney, a Bradford accountant, has produced 1,000 of the badges.

" I saw the badge in the Family Doctor," he told The Yorkshire Post, " but that design did not have any lettering on it, so I put a message on."

Mr. Hockney, who said that he had the support of an eminent Leeds chest specialist, hopes to sell the badges to children for 6d. each. " The surplus will go to the anti-smoking campaign.

" I would like teachers to participate in the distribution of the badges by telling the children of the dangers of smoking.

" The British Government still refuses to act against this acknowledged killer," he said at his Hutton-Terrace, Eccleshill, home.

" Smoking and cancer, especially of the lung, are directly linked, of that there can be no further doubt.

" Good health is worth more than a fortune. To encourage children and young people to be non-smokers, this badge has been produced."

The anti-smoking badge

Dec 21/64

A man ahead of his time?

I was still doing my two jobs. In one memorable week I was alerted three nights running by staff on the next ward because I had not heard babies crying in the nursery opposite my office. So I went to have my ears syringed. There was no wax. That is when I had a full hearing check and was found to be quite deaf. I saw the Ear, Nose and Throat specialist. 'Yes you are deaf and it will get worse,' he said. 'It is sensori-neural hearing loss caused by damage to the inner ear or to the nerves that send sound to the brain. A hearing aid might help.'

I was supplied with a Medresco hearing-aid from the National Health Service, named after the Medical Research Council. It was as big as a cigarette box and had a length of wire to the ear-mould. There was a clip to fix on a belt or a pocket. As a bonus they offered me a pouch with a neck strap. I heard every crackle of my starched nurse's apron, paper, cutlery, traffic, wind, clothing, body sounds, children screaming, whistling, clopping shoe-heels and other dreadful noises. Music and radio became painful sounds through those aids. But I couldn't hear voices properly. I had to constantly fiddle with the volume control because it was too loud, too soft or not clear enough.

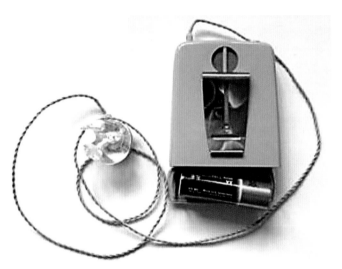

Medresco hearing aid issued by NHS in 1966.

It was early 1966 and I was thirty. I was told that commercial hearing- aids were the way to go, but they were expensive. Good thing I had two jobs because I spent all my savings on a pair that were certainly more convenient to wear than the NHS one; but there was still a lot of extra background noise and whistling. It was very difficult to hear voices.

Pauline and I had been getting itchy feet and scanning the Nursing Times for jobs abroad. We had sent for details about 'working in the sunshine for twelve months'. It was Zambian sunshine and we had already submitted application forms. I told her to go alone or pal up with someone else. She said I might as well go for the interview if we were called. We were called, so we went for a medical and X-ray in Harley Street, London, then for the interview. I felt miserable having to explain about my hearing problem. Back in Harrogate, I was trying to come to terms with a major change in my life away from nursing.

Surprise, surprise, through the letterbox: 'I am pleased to inform you that your application has been successful'. So I was going to Zambia; but I was also going deaf. I tried to work out the cause and reached two possible explanations: psychological, maybe I was trying to not hear my mother; or the condition had been caused by the ECT treatment I had in Australia. Then a likelier truth dawned on me:

deafness was genetic on both sides of the family. Although my mother had the most astute hearing right until she died aged ninety-eight, her sisters, and nephews wore hearing-aids. Also my father and many of his family had hearing-aids when quite young; his mother was very deaf. Eventually three of my brothers needed hearing-aids. If we didn't speak up, Dad didn't hear what we said, so we all spoke quite loudly, except Mum who always spoke softly. I was now having trouble hearing what she said.

After both Mum and Dad had died I read Mum's diaries. There was not a single mention of my deafness, as though she thought hearing-aids were as effective as wearing glasses. In 1954 Mum had written a letter (and kept a copy) to *Family Doctor*, the popular medical magazine of the day. It surprised me to learn that Dad must have had hearing problems since the time I was born. This is what she wrote: -

About 20 years ago — the firm where my husband worked started using adding machines. He said he could not stand the noise and plugged his ears with cotton wool soaked in olive oil. Not only did he do this at work, but continued at home. We had 5 children as time went on, my husband still continued with his plugging for several years. He continually complained of deafness and has attended clinics, hospitals and even a private doctor — all as an outpatient. He has deaf aids, with which he will not persevere. Now our family are growing up and are annoyed because Dad hears when he shouldn't but not when he should. I have heard of deaf people like that but I wonder if there is anything in it. Most music he does not like, especially the chapel organ, and the family often have to switch off the wireless for him.

I have tried to be patient all these years and often repeat things 3 or 4 times. My husband will not try to lip-read and thinks I am wrong if I get impatient. His jealousies and suspicions have grown and everyone is wrong but himself. I sometimes wonder if I have been too soft and patient with him, or is it possible that a selfish, fault-finding life can grow from being hard of hearing. I feel that only a change of heart can make a difference — Please enlighten.

Family Doctor sent a kind and courteous reply, summarising that maybe she needed, 'a change of heart to bring about the change she hoped for'.

That letter and reply were lodged in her diary of 1954. This made me realise how hard the condition must have been for both of them. No wonder Dad didn't like the Chapel organ. He would have had terrible background noises in those early hearing-aids, and Mum would not have had the quiet contemplative talks and closeness that she craved and felt denied.

As for lip-reading, I did go to some classes but found it difficult. Eventually I could not hear in the dark because I needed to see the face, so I must have been lip-reading without knowing it. Also I stopped watching television unless the programme had sub-titles, which were few and far between. Back in 1966 when I told Mum and Dad about my deafness, Dad offered some of his experience with hearing-aids whilst Mum seemed to think I was ganging up with him. She still didn't believe in deafness and had no idea of how difficult it was to hear through the hearing-aids.

Our flight to Zambia was scheduled for October. As usual Mum was short of cash, so before leaving I gave her an extra month's pay for board. I had been giving her two pounds a week even when I didn't live at home. I could not really afford the extra eight pounds. Mum still cried a lot and though I know Dad was not easy, she couldn't seem to accept the way he was. I let all my brothers know that if anything happened to Mum, I would look after Dad. I whispered to myself, God help me if Dad dies first, not sure that I could look after Mum.

11 Africa

On October 24, 1964, Zambia became independent from British rule. Prime Minister Kenneth Kaunda became the inaugural president. We arrived two years later in October 1966, employed as nurse-midwives by the Zambian Government. By the end of our contract (which was extended to three years), we should have helped to teach Zambian nurses and midwives to work independently.

A week after arrival in Ndola, Pauline and I had agonisingly sun-burned shoulders; folded handkerchiefs were taped under our uniforms to stop friction and help us to get on with the work. We had discovered that October was 'suicide month' in Zambia, the sun scorching the earth and its creatures waiting for the rain season to offer respite. Our rooms were around an open courtyard; inside and outside were hot as Hades, which made the sight of an adjoining swimming-pool all the more tempting as a place to spend all our off-duty. Now our shoulders were bearing the brunt of the relentless sun. We wore the white uniforms that had seemed appropriate when we bought them in England, but soon realised why we needed at least five of them. At the end of a shift they were crumpled with sweat, our white lightweight shoes and white stockings offered no protection from the heat rising

Children's bath. Isolation Ward, Kasama Hospital, Zambia, 1966. Cold water and carbolic soap.

from the ground. The wards were hot too, with no air-conditioning except for two large ceiling fans spinning the hot air and cooling it very slightly. Patients with fever or malaria would have their beds moved under the fans, with cold wet sheets wrung out to cool them. Flies were everywhere; it was fly paradise. We just had to get used to the flies and the heat.

We only stayed two weeks in Ndola before flying three-hundred miles to Kasama in the Northern Province. The flight was hot, bumpy, with an overpowering smell of blue grass perfume mixed with body odours. We refused the sandwiches and drinks for fear of being sick. We felt giddy and ill, not daring to move until three hours later when we arrived and were met and driven to our new abode, the Sister's mess. There were three other sisters and three houseboys who did the cleaning, gardening and cooking.

The house was more than a mile from the hospital. There were five of us with a room each and a shared kitty to buy food. Fresh meat, vegetables, butter and eggs were scarce in the shops; there were hardly any potatoes or flour. Our gardener grew vegetables and salad. There was no fresh milk; we had to make it up from powder. Insects were myriad despite the fly-wires covering the windows and doors. If food was not covered it would soon be swarming with flying ants, beetles, flies, bluebottles and goodness knows what else. I quickly had to inform Mum that mail was only collected and delivered twice a week by the plane that brought meat and supplies for the hospital and few local shops. In the garden were bananas, mangos, guavas, passion fruit, and pawpaw, as well as the beautiful smelling frangipane.

Poinsettia trees on Golf Course Road, Kasama.

Poinsettia trees lined the dirt road that led to the golf course and the club. I soon fell in love with Africa, the colours, the climate and the local Bemba people. The primitive living and lack of shops tuned us so much more into nature.

There were many working emigrants: teachers, lawyers, government

officers, bank boys, agronomists, all in all a happy friendly place, despite the discomforts and poor working conditions. We were transported back and forth to work by Land Rover. We were warned not to walk because of the danger of snakes. If we did walk in long grass, we were told to walk heavily and noisily to hopefully frighten off any such reptiles.

There were two hospitals: fee-paying and non-fee-paying. Fee-paying had eight beds and an out-patient clinic. It was similar to the Australian Bush hospitals, catering for anything at all and was used for patients who earned more than an agreed amount. The more they were paid, the higher the fee. To be eligible for fee-paying admission or out-patient visits, blue cards were issued. No blue card meant the maximum fee was charged.

The non-fee-paying hospital was at first a shock. There were on average two hundred beds, but three hundred or more patients; lots of them were nursed on the floor between the beds, or even outside under the trees. There were wards for men, women and children. At the far end was Isolation, consisting of a few scattered wards and an outside zinc bath for bathing children. Isolated patients were adults and children with leprosy, TB, whooping cough, measles, typhoid, and other tropical diseases. Most of the children were mal-nourished too. Measles especially could prove fatal.

Hospital staff consisted of one matron, four doctors, nine of us nursing sisters and, on each ward, two or three medical assistants covering the twenty-four hour shifts. There were also 'dressers' who were called to help as non-trained staff.

On our first day three deaths occurred in the hospital, which was not particularly unusual. But each death was accompanied by a group of family and friends, mainly women who wailed loudly as the bodies were taken to the mortuary. The wailing would continue outside the mortuary for hours, it seemed to me like all day long. The noise played havoc with my hearing-aids, causing whistling and the need to adjust them. Family and friends of patients all camped around the hospital with their household luggage and cooking equipment tied in a bag and carried on their head or shoulders. You got used to the wailing because it happened pretty well every day.

There were even more flies than at Ndola — in the luggage, on the beds, in the noses, on the food, in the cups of drinks, in the eyes and lips of the very sick, and around most of the children. There was a poor patient with severe burns from lightning, whose bed was covered with a mosquito net, but attracted such a swarm of flies they pushed the net down onto her and laid eggs on her burned body. We extracted maggots nearly half-an-inch long.

By December routines were becoming familiar, but staff changes were happening constantly. We would swing from being under-staffed with doctors or nurses, to being well-staffed. We thought the hospital would be too busy and over-crowded for Christmas decorations, but the hospital secretary surprised us on Christmas Eve by delivering a massive Christmas tree and fixing it firmly at the entrance to the long outdoor hospital corridor. There were baubles and tinsel and shining streamers, a few angels and stars. We all helped to trim it up whilst many patients sat around the patchy grass watching. A couple of Christmas carols completed the celebration. We bade good night and, 'A Merry Christmas', to the patients as transport drove us home.

Next morning, full of Christmas spirit and knowing 'tis better to give than to receive', I was flabbergasted to see the tree: totally naked, stripped of all the decorations and branches broken off. The Hospital Secretary met us, aware that we would be shocked. 'Merry Christmas', he said and waved his arms in all directions where the families were camping with their bundles. They were all trimmed up, a bauble on a tree branch here, streamer there, angels, stars. Smiling faces and clasped hands bowed as we surveyed them. 'Thank you, Merry Christmas', they chanted. Yes of course: we gave, they took.

There were small Christmas gifts for patients. Each received a packet containing one bar of Lifebuoy soap; a quarter-pound packet of sugar; a packet of six biscuits; a toothbrush and a two-ounce packet of tea. That was given to more than three hundred patients. They were most grateful as they closed their hands and bowed their heads to thank us. There were smiles of pleasure even amongst the very ill: quite humbling really for such a small and almost insignificant gift.

There was plenty to write home about. I wrote so much that my brother Paul, the local preacher, had some letters printed-out with a request for clothing for cool nights resulting in five parcels of beautiful clothes for adults and children. The first parcel we took to the long-stay patients with tuberculosis or leprosy in Isolation Wards. They had a great time choosing what they liked and dressing up the children. It made a change from the hospital uniforms that were navy blue cotton twill bearing the words Kasama Hospital. Two weeks later nobody was

wearing their new clothes. The relatives of the patients had sold them
and bought cigarettes or chibuku, a potent local beer. When the next
four boxes arrived, we told our house-boys that we would be having a
sale, so they could tell their friends, most of whom lived in nice mud
huts. We also told the hospital staff. The buyers were like vultures,
buying all they could afford at bargain prices. We had the sale on a
Saturday so they hadn't had time to spend yesterday's pay on chibuku.
We made nearly £20 (approximately £260 in 2016) from the first sale,
and got a seamstress to make bright new uniforms for the children's
ward. We continued with the fund-raising and by the next Christmas
included a scarf in the women's gifts, a handkerchief for the men, and
a soft toy for the children. Mum still wanted more letters and a morn-
to-night description of my days, so in a generous mood I wrote this
true verbatim account:

The day of Sunday December 4, 1966.

*Arrived on duty 8 am, my colleague was at church (RC), and joined me
at 9am.*

* *8 am: Ambulance drove to airport for a woman with snakebite,
meanwhile a woman in labour arrived, and a man with cellulitis to be
admitted. Snakebite lady arrived. She had to lie on the floor, as there was
no empty bed.*

* *8.30 am: Collect the list of patients from medical assistant or dresser on
each ward, and work out how much food is required for the day. There
were 324 patients, each to have 10 ounces of rice (light diet) or 10 ounces
of mealie meal (regular diet), 4 ounces of beans, 2 ounces of peanuts, half
ounce of sugar, one and half ounce dried fish (kapenta), one and half
ounce dried milk (half pint). Go to kitchen do the maths and supervise
weighing of food.*

* *10 am: Help other sister to make extra milk drinks for special sick
patients, and distribute it. Another two snakebites came with very
inflamed legs. A woman with severe infection of abdomen arrived, and
a 2 month old child with convulsions.*

* *11 am: should be coffee time, but the woman in labour had her baby.
Quick cup of coffee at 11.40am, broken off by admission of a woman in a
rigor with malaria, and a one year old child who swallowed a whole fish.*

Another child came on his mother's back (as they all are), with scabies. She had carried him 40 miles, slept in the bush last night. One of the patients with snakebite then had an epileptic fit, and 3 more minor cases arrived on female ward.

• 12 noon: A boy of 16 came in with septicaemia from a buffalo gore, but died two hours later. I accompanied Doctor to assess these new patients, and give prescribed treatments. When I did the count for food weighing, I noticed on Isolation wards there were 46 patients with TB, 14 with leprosy, 14 children have measles, two of them have cerebral complications and sadly will die, 4 have whooping cough. Giving out medicines, food, delivering babies, dealing with casualties and giving treatment is non-stop from going on duty to finishing.

The weather is very hot and close today. There has been no rain for 2 days and we are feeling the effect. President Kaunda and his wife are coming to Kasama on Friday so we may see them. His mother is a patient in Fee Paying hospital. They are doing a tour of the hospital, I hope they bring pegs for the nose, it gets so smelly! Vastly overcrowded. On female ward of thirty six beds today there were fifty-one patients, so you can imagine under and over the bed. Add to this at least one relative for each patient, who feeds them, gives them water, bedpans, and washes them, so there is constant movement as they walk up and down. Also being female ward, 12 or more have a baby in bed with them; there are dozens of flies to each person, and more around their bags of luggage.

Finished work at 2 pm.

Flies and insects are rampant. They make a tremendous noise too. There are no windows round Fee Paying hospital, just mosquito wire netting, and nearly every inch gets covered with insects of all shapes and sizes, they are attracted by the lights inside the hospital. I managed to kill a big buzzing moth which I swatted, and it collided in a doped state with a baby mouse on the floor. The mouse was smaller than the moth and disappeared while I gave another swat to the moth. I hate killing things, but it is awful when they get inside the wards at Fee Paying. The variety of insects is unbelievable, Praying mantis, cockroaches, beetles, spiders, ants, mosquitoes, and many that I don't know the names of. It is a constant battle to keep them outside and not in the building. The natives actually collect flying ants in tin cans when they creep under doors and

President Kaunda visited
Kasama Hospital 1967.

before they fly away. They cook them as a delicacy. And no, I haven't tried them!

Yesterday Pauline and I went on tour with one of the doctors, unusual for us to both manage the same day off, so we made the most of it. We went to a small dispensary 50 miles away on a very rough bumpy road, in a mud hut village. Terribly inadequate, there is one medical assistant and 3 huts are his whole hospital for about 900 patients a year. Doctor visits once a month, and anyone very serious or in need of surgery are given a voucher to go to Kasama on board the bus. Kasama is the capital of the Northern Province, the full medical quota is seven doctors, four of them based in Kasama. They cover over half a million people.

We took lessons to learn Bemba, the local tribal language. At least we learnt enough to help patients feel at ease when they were admitted, asking them basic details in their own tongue. My deafness was more of a nuisance socially than on the wards because of the foreign language. We were not really expected to understand answers to our questions. Patients would reply to a dresser or other native staff who could interpret for us.

Socially, deafness was a different matter. We would have dinners or events with teachers, bank-boys and anyone around really. There was a local pub-type club for larger events and I was even in a play — only a small part but I had to get someone to cue me when my turn came. A local teacher gave a dinner party for about twelve of us. We sat around a large round table. There was background music from arriving to leaving and we stayed about four hours. The music muffled speech, so I had no idea what the topics of conversation were. All I could do was copy the facial expressions around me; nobody realised that I could not hear anything. I discovered that most people are quite happy to hear their own voice; but it was a long and boring event, and my face ached with trying to look interested.

I managed to buy a five-year-old Volkswagen Beetle from a school-teacher who was leaving. It was the colour of red sand like the one in Australia. Trouble was that petrol rationing only allowed coupons for between five and ten gallons a month, which would only take us a on round trip of a hundred-and-fifty to three hundred miles; but at least we could get to the shops and market in Kasama. We would save petrol ready for longer trips. However, I did manage to go with a colleague to Lake Tanganyika. We travelled five hundred miles in three days, which isn't really far, but the roads were poor. Either we drove through sand drifts, bricks dislodged in the rain season, or for the most part hard-corrugated sand. After the first ten miles we got used to the noise and jerks. The car made the trip all right and it was a nice change to see the Lake.

I didn't get as many photos as I would have liked, because there was nowhere in Kasama to process them. Black-and-white films sent to Ndola took six weeks to return; colour slides to Johannesburg took six-to-eight weeks. Some got lost. The medical assistant in X-ray at hospital did some black-and-white processing when he had time, but he was too busy really. I even sent some films home for Dad to develop and print. A notice of a photography class was put up at the club. I joined and learned how to develop my own. The teacher ordered developing equipment for us to buy and hired an enlarger for printing. We could only do black-and-white, but it was useful and I still posted colour slides off to Johannesburg.

One of the first photos I processed and proudly sent to Mum and Dad probably shocked them. It was a print of a baby with two heads. The mother had arrived in second stage of labour. It was a breech presenting, but there was an obstruction. The foetal heart was normal, surprisingly, because she had walked several miles. We thought it was hydrocephalus or locked twins. She might need a Caesarian but theatre was not free at the time. Doctor tried to disengage the 'lock' and the baby finally delivered normally, but one of the necks was broken at birth so of course it was a stillborn two-headed baby.

Another patient walked twelve miles with an obstructed second stage of labour. We delivered her twins at 5 am, but they were both stillborn. Three hours later she was discharged and set off on the walk back home carrying the dead twins in a cloth. Her husband walked in front, the custom being that he was not allowed to touch them, as they might be a curse. So the mother carried them home. He dug the hole and she buried them.

The women were very strong; most of the carrying was on their back and on their head. Often they had a big tin trunk on their head, I don't know what was inside, but flies were attracted to it. One woman who had been axed through the skull in a domestic tiff walked six miles to the hospital carrying her baby on her back and fed him at the breast throughout her short stay in hospital. Relatives of the sick would camp around the hospital, foraging for food and maybe offer us mushrooms to buy.

One thing Kasama taught people was patience. If there were no eggs or mail on Monday's plane, one just waited until Thursday when there would still probably be no eggs or mail. Patients walked miles in labour or severely-ill or carrying sick relatives. This totally different way of life made the hectic life going on in towns easy to forget.

I was writing long letters full of news, yet Mum kept saying she was not getting enough. Her complaint didn't bother me anymore. I pointed out that I too did not get many letters, sometimes they came in twos or threes, mail was very erratic. I told her: 'A friend received a letter last week to say her father had died one week ago, but she had never received the three telegrams sent the week before, so she will probably receive them eventually.'

We spent eighteen months in Kasama and asked for a transfer to Lusaka, to compare the different towns and ways of life. Pauline had met Colin, who was working in Kasama in the office of the Resident

Mushroom sellers near the hospital. The Alice in Wonderland mushrooms were enormous — but tasty, I was assured.

Secretary. By the end of our three years in Zambia they were married. I was saving up petrol ready to drive to Lusaka when our transfer came through.

Finally in April, 1968, Pauline and I left Kasama to travel to Lusaka. I drove in the Volkswagen Beetle, although no one thought the car would make it. We left 5 am Tuesday for the five-hundred mile drive, the last one-hundred-and-fifty being the only good road. We had no major catastrophes and carried thirteen gallons of spare petrol with us, filling up the car every hundred miles. The road in parts was very rough, but we arrived at Broken Hill (Kabwe), eighty-five miles from Lusaka by 6 pm. We thought that we were going to be late, arriving at a new hospital, so we spent the night at Broken Hill hospital and finished the last eighty-five miles on Wednesday morning.

When we first arrived in Zambia, the currency was the British pound. The pound had a similar value to Britain. In 1968 it changed to decimal using the Zambian kwacha and ngwee. One kwacha was equal to one hundred ngwee. When the kwacha was introduced it was equivalent to half the Zambian pound — ten shillings. We scrutinised our payslips, which looked as though our wage had doubled, but soon got used to the value of the new currency.

12 Sick African Children

'Please Sir. I'd like some more' Children's
Ward, Lusaka hospital, 1968.

Lusaka Hospital was a shock. Another overcrowded hospital: over half
a mile of scattered buildings. However, a brand new hospital was being
built that included a new maternity unit and training schools for
medical students, nurses and pupil-midwives.

    We were fortunate that a new block of single purpose-built flats were
available for nursing sisters, fully-furnished and well-equipped with
linen, crockery, cutlery and even an iron and ironing-board. All I had
to get was a fridge; in the relentless heat milk would turn sour and
butter rancid within an hour. I planted pots of vegetables and tomatoes
on the balcony. We could walk to the hospital and then into town.
Pauline and I spent the first day shopping. With all the food in the

shops it was hard to believe we were in the same country as Kasama. We noticed how the girls in the dining room moaned about silly things regarding food. We said nothing, but ate everything and looked forward to city life.

I worked on the children's medical ward was which was over-crowded. The upper age limit was five-years-old, so a-six-year old would be admitted to an adult ward. There were fifteen cots for babies up to about six months of age. We got regular cases of tetanus due to infection of the umbilical cord in babies born at home or in the bush. Those who arrived too late for tetanus vaccine would have fits of going rigid (lock jaw) and inevitably died. We saw babies with gastro-enteritis, causing dehydration and others with pneumonia. The cots were always occupied, but at least half of those babies would not survive.

In the main Children's ward were forty cots, another three in a side-room were reserved for barrier nursing of infectious diseases. All children were labelled round the wrist with their name, cot number, date of admission and diagnosis. No matter how busy we were, record-keeping was a high priority in nursing care. There would be two or even three children in one cot. They might grab each other's drips and feeding tubes, sometimes pulling them out. It could be hard to know which ones had diarrhoea or round-worms. Children with sickle cell anaemia could have severe pains; we tried to make sure they had a cot to themselves.

Every child was bathed each morning whilst the cot linen was changed. Most would be undressed, sitting on the floor to wait their turn. In the infection room we put carbolic mixture in bowls or buckets, into which damp carbolic sheets would hang over screens round each isolated cot.

There were terrible cases of malnutrition. Those with marasmus looked like skeletons and would usually be under three-years-old and be very undernourished and dehydrated. Other children might have kwashiorkor, a protein calorie malnutrition that was an enigma to uneducated parents. Mothers would make bracelets of beads for their babies; as the wrist grew more beads were added and mother would presume her baby was thriving. If the diet was lacking protein, with the child having too much cassava cereal, they could contract kwashiorkor. Their little bodies would become distended with fluid, so the plump wrist was not a sign of thriving but of malnutrition.

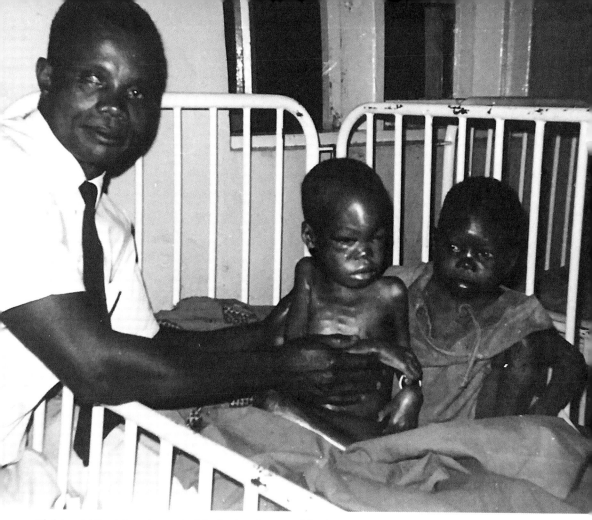

Children's Ward, Lusaka 1968. Medical assistant is blind in one eye since childhood illness. One child in cot has kwashiorkor.

There would be new admissions, discharges and deaths daily. Knowing every individual child was impossible; but I remember one little boy that I admitted when his mother arrived on the ward, carrying him on her back.

His skin was a mass of sores on his limp, waterlogged little body that was suffering from kwashiorkor. His mouth and nose startled me - just one big raw area, discharging and attracting flies. He was called Mwambi. At first we fed him through a vein in his scalp. We didn't really expect him to live, but he had his own survival ideas and gradually improved. Improvement brought fear and awareness. He would wail incessantly with a high-pitched cry whenever we changed his clothes or cleaned his discharging nose, mouth and eyes. He had not yet learnt to talk or walk although he was four years old. When we finally took his drip down and gave him food by mouth, his mouth was healed but it had become round and small, so that we couldn't insert a spoon. Mwambi would push his tongue onto a handful of food and eat it his own way. We always taught children to eat with spoons because of the dangers of being fed through a dirty bottle or dirty teat. Even tiny babies were spoon-fed if their mothers were unable to breast-feed them. We were teaching parents as well as caring for their children.

Mwambi's mother, along with other mothers, was taught how to provide a more healthy diet and how to watch for signs of illness. We asked healthy fathers to give blood for their malnourished child. Mwambi's father agreed to donate a pint of blood. He was also advised how to budget his small income and arrange his garden to feed his family and keep them healthy. Little Mwambi was on the ward for three months by which time he could walk a few steps, although he would crawl if he had the chance. He finally ate his dinner with a spoon. The emergence of a few teeth and a delightful smile on his newly-healed face endeared him to all the staff. He was discharged in September along with many other children. My memory of him would no doubt have faded if I hadn't noticed him again at Christmas.

By December I had moved from Children's ward and was working on the busy maternity ward, but during lunch-break on Christmas Day I went to visit my old ward to see the tree and decorations. These were very scant as most of the young patients were too ill to notice festivities or were quite bewildered by it all. Whilst chatting to colleagues I felt an urgent tug on my uniform. At first I didn't recognise him, but then, suddenly, 'eureka' that brave little smile could never be forgotten: it was Mwambi. At the ward door, proudly watching him, were his mother and father. Mwambi was chattering away in his own language, his eyes rapt intently on the Christmas tree. He clutched with delight the small toy we gave him — from a tub full of donated toys. His parents looked shyly guilty as they called him. Many parents brought their children to see Christmas at the hospital, but I didn't recognise any of the others. As Mwambi waved goodbye I realised that the toy he tightly held was probably the only one he had ever had; but I was also aware that he had been given the gift of hope in his young life, now that his parents had no fear of the hospital and were learning ways to keep their family healthy.

In 1968 I worked on Maternity during Christmas. There were eighteen babies born on Christmas day and night, so we were busy as

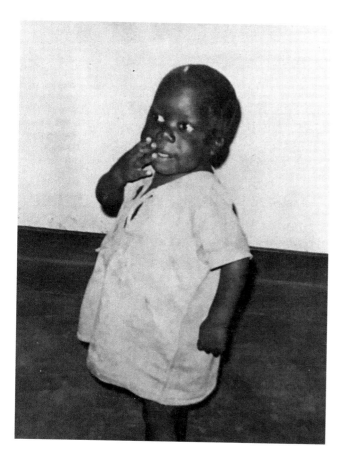

Little Mwambi
when he visited
the hospital on
Christmas Day.

always. There were only seven beds in labour ward, a T-shaped room. Many were having babies on the floor, laid on red rubber mackintoshes. We had to walk over them after we had scrubbed our hands in the one sink. Some births were easy, but there were many complications. Emergencies would arrive bleeding before or after delivery. Things that the textbooks had told us we might never see — we saw them. Ruptured uterus, severe anaemia, infection, obstructed labour, toxaemia, retained placenta. There would also be risks to the newborn: maybe a malnourished or exhausted mother with inadequate foetal nutrition, prolonged labour before admission causing foetal distress. Prematurity and malformations were common. The maternal and neonatal death-rate was sadly quite high.

We had no pediatrician, unless we called him specifically. There was a tilted board on which to place the newborn baby for mucous extraction and to record the Apgar score, which assessed their normality or risks. We name-labelled each child before the cord was cut and then swaddled the newborn in a cotton blanket. There were twelve wooden pigeon-holes lined with washable plastic mattresses built into one wall where we slotted the babies until mother was ready to go to the post-natal ward with her child.

There were always twice as many mothers as beds in the lying-in ward, therefore patients with complications had the beds; most of the others slept on the floor. We had a few incubators for premature and sick babies and about twenty cots in the nursery for recovering or malformed babies. There were over nine thousand babies born in the previous year. Mum was still complaining she was not getting enough letters, so I just kept writing about how busy we were.

I was looking forward to working in the new maternity hospital due to open a couple of months before my contract ended. It would be good to compare it with the appalling conditions in which we were working. The midwifery tutor was also looking forward to teaching pupil-midwives, but did not want them to start in the old hospital. I couldn't blame her for that. The experience might put them off midwifery forever. Quite often labour ward sounded like a cattle shed with the poor labouring mothers pushing and breathing loudly. There were constant invasions of new patients. Either they walked in, or were brought by ambulance on stretchers. They could be extremely ill, in need of urgent care on a bed. It was quite common for a labouring mother to have to give up her bed, even in second stage of labour, and deliver on the floor. Those mothers never complained, especially when their new baby cried lustily. They didn't mind that they were shuffled around to make room for urgent cases.

I worked several months on night duty in Out-Patients, at the far end of the hospital near the mothers' hostel. That was for mothers who

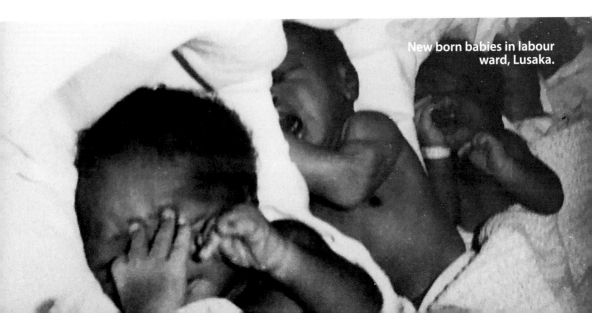

New born babies in labour ward, Lusaka.

were feeding their premature or sick babies. They got a mattress and
food. Every three hours, day and night, a bell rang to alert them to
feeding time. Almost every night the sound of wailing echoed outside
the hostel — that meant death of a child. Some nights there were four
or five deaths. The flats we lived in were on the path from the hospital
and Pauline said she was wakened most nights by these wailers passing
by. I didn't hear them at night with my hearing aids out but it was like
a moaning song and was quite unmistakable.

Out-Patients was a further education. I never knew how much
violence there was between friends. In their friendly fights they broke
beer bottles on each other's head, making deep wounds with lots of
bleeding. Sometimes they came with axe wounds, flesh marked with
iron bars, kicks, or even human bites — big deep ones that needed
stitching.

We averaged forty out-patients a night, a third of which were police
cases. There would always be a queue of sick children as well as adults.
The staff comprised of two medical assistants and myself, plus cleaners-
cum-porters. There was a doctor on call for the whole hospital. If he
got too busy we would have to recruit the second on call. The Out-
Patient building was modern and up-to-date with equipment, which
was a great help.

A lot of street and towns were changing to Zambian names.
Southern Rhodesia, as it was then called, was under the regime of white
Prime Minister Ian Smith, who made the Unilateral Declaration of
Independence after negotiating with British Prime Minister Harold
Wilson in 1965. This caused tension and rebellion because it meant that
two hundred and twenty thousand white Rhodesians would have

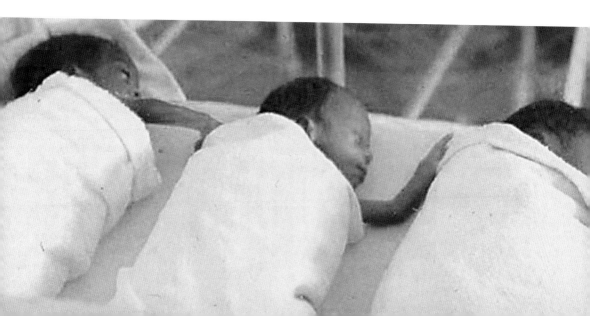

privileges and rule over four million black Rhodesians. Eventually, twelve years after we left Africa, Robert Mugabe was elected Prime Minister of an independent Zimbabwe under a new constitution. I was not familiar with the politics, but when daily life was affected one had to learn a little about the tensions. Black trained nurses coming to work in Lusaka from South Africa on a one-way ticket out of the land of their birth made us acutely aware of the apartheid system. But there was no conflict in Zambia: we worked as great teams in the hospitals and made many friends of all colours and ranks.

In July 1968 Pauline and I, with two other friends, spent ten days travelling around Rhodesia. Colin suggested we drove his car, a large comfortable Wolseley, as it was more spacious than my VW. He was temporarily working in Nairobi. I drove all the way, about fifteen hundred miles in all. We stayed in Salisbury (Harare) for two nights, a lovely city much bigger than Lusaka. Then we spent two nights at Lake McIlwaine (Lake Chivero), a restful little place, before going to Inyanga for two nights, a picturesque mountainous area with ancient ruins, slave pits, streams and pine forests. All unchanged since the Stone Age I'd say: miles and miles of no habitation, but beautiful scenery. We spent the last two nights at Leopard Rock Hotel in the Bvumba Mountain, the hotel where the Queen Mother and Princess Margaret stayed. Bvumba means mist and the mountains were continually mingled with balls of mist. Although the hills were cold the sun shone every day, and we all felt better for the change of air.

Two months after the Rhodesia trip the Volkswagen car steering-wheel came off in my hands. Two months passed before it was fixed. I got a new chassis head, a very expensive job, but cheaper than another second-hand car. Wear and tear was no doubt due to so much driving in the bush on bad roads. I was lucky that it happened at the hospital. Meanwhile I joined Pauline and another friend in their car for five days down at Livingstone and Victoria Falls.

We crossed the bridge to Rhodesia. I had never been over before but the experience was worth it. Victoria Falls was beautiful. There were rainbows everywhere as sunlight poured through the water. The pity was that the border of Zambia and Rhodesia was right in the middle. There was a bridge with a white line in the centre to which one could walk from either country; to go further required passport formalities. We only spent ten hours on the Rhodesian side, but it was a lovely trip.

Not a photo-journalist on assignment but me, on holiday 1968.

Victoria Falls, Zambia.

My final exciting drive in the VW in April, 1969, was planned with a friend I met in Kasama. Sickness and staff holidays meant they couldn't make it, so I decided to go alone, a drive of about fifteen hundred miles to Durban in South Africa. Pauline and Colin were in Salisbury for a week celebrating their engagement. I spent two nights with them before continuing on my great adventure. I took two days to reach Salisbury. I thought the rain season was ended, but a torrential storm threatened my windscreen wipers which could only work very slowly. I had to stop and sleep in the car about eighty miles from Salisbury.

The route to Johannesburg was via Beit Bridge. Just as I left, the rain started pelting again. When dusk fell I discovered my headlights were not working properly, so I pulled into Louis Trichardt for the night and continued early next morning. As I avoided driving in the dark or heavy rain, the journey to Johannesburg and the edge of the Drakensberg Mountains took three days. There were some very long uninhabited roads with a tar strip in the middle and dirt on the edges for passing, although I scarcely met anything to pass either way. In fact for about a hundred miles there were just baboons and me, quite a lot of large baboons that could be dangerous. I had to drive carefully and I did not stop. I was lucky not to get stuck with those baboons because the car broke down about every hundred miles. It ground to a halt with no help in sight. I had a little camping gas stove, water, dried milk and coffee. I boiled water and made a coffee and hoped the car would start again. Luck was on my side because the car spluttered into life after about an hour's wait. I knew there was a problem with the lights and the wipers, but hoped to reach Durban to get the car fixed. As I reached South Africa I was treated to the most wonderful flora. Proteas, red flowering aloes and other glorious exotic flowers growing wild, contrasted with the ever-changing greenery and mountain ranges. I finally arrived in Durban and once settled in a hotel, took the car to be serviced. When I went to collect it the foreman thought I had had a fire in the engine, there were so many burnt wires. They were all renewed, ready for the return journey.

Pauline flew down from Salisbury and we spent a few days on the Durban beach before driving back to Lusaka together. We drove with well-functioning lights and windscreen wipers and camped in a circular tent at the Matapos national park near Bulawayo; then for two nights in a well-equipped tent at Victoria Falls National Park. We saw

warthogs, elephants and hippos, around Victoria Falls and the Zambezi
River. The holiday left us fully restored and ready to get back to work.
I took no chances with the car as I had driven over a thousand miles
on all types of roads since Durban. I took it for a local service, but there
were no problems. What a faithful little car that was.

On September 2, Pauline flew home to England, planning to marry
Colin in October. After seeing her off, I had an all-inclusive trip from
Lusaka to Kafue Safari Park. With fellow travellers I flew to Ngoma,
where we were picked up for a Landrover tour. About ten of us were
'caged' in the back of the vehicle and travelled towards our camp for
the night frighteningly close to lions, kudos, buffalo and zebra. Next
morning we were shown a hippo that had been killed by a lion
(according to our guide). I was glad not to see the kill happening. The
hippo was massive. We ventured on a boat trip on the Kafue River and
were told there were leopards and cheetahs. We saw rhinoceroses and
impala. In the dark evening we returned to the dead hippo and saw by
moonlight an amazing sight. There was scarcely any flesh left on the
animal, wild dogs were taking chunks of flesh and vultures were
swooping inside the carcass to feed themselves. The lions would have
had their share, but we didn't see them. As there was only skin and
head left we realized that many creatures must have fed from it.

Work was busier than ever on maternity ward; but the new
Maternity Hospital was ready to be opened on October 1. My contract
was nearly ended and I had booked my passage home on October 26.
I was so pleased to have the opportunity to move into the new hospital.
There was a separate antenatal ward; complicated pregnancies were no
longer to be nursed on the same ward as post-natal mothers. Fantastic
new labour wards, well-furnished and equipped, included containers
for patients' luggage, so the wards should remain cleaner with fewer
flies. Everything about it was new and wonderful. We didn't all move
from the old unit. Gradually patients were discharged home from the
old one whilst new patients were admitted to the new building.

The official opening by President Kaunda was on October 23, the
day before Independence Day. I enjoyed both celebrations and next
day I was gone. Ten of my colleagues took me to the airport where we
enjoyed a goodbye lunch. I flew to Nairobi for three nights at New
Stanley Hotel and then got the night train to Mombasa in a comfortable sleeper carriage to spend four nights at Dolphin Hotel Mombasa,
which was on a white-sanded beach. I left Mombasa on a smallish ship,

the *Kampala*, British India Line. Ports of calls were all delayed with slow loading of cargo, so there was chance to tour at Dar-es-Salam, Beira, Lorenco Marques before arriving in Durban ready to board the *Oranje* on the Union Castle Line. After stops at East London, Port Elizabeth, Capetown and the Canary Islands, we finally we docked in Southampton at 8 am on December 1, 1969.

Mum and Dad had been having their own excitement. Early in January, Philip invited them to Australia. David had volunteered help finance the adventure. Mum worried about Dad and his diabetes, but David said, 'Don't worry think of the grandchildren you will see.' Mum also worried that he was spending too much on their trip, but he said not to worry, 'money is to use.'

So on March 28, 1969, Mum and Dad set sail on *The Aranda* for Australia. David presented Mum with an instamatic camera and gave film to Dad for the journey, plus tips on how to go about things on the

Mum and Dad in their cabin sailing to Australia.

ship, such as gratuities and shore excursions where natives might beg for cash. 'Give them some if you take their photos,' he said.

Their cabin had three windows and ample wardrobes, bed lights and press-buttons for attendance. Very comfy. It was the ship's first voyage under the Shaw Saville Line.

Mum's diary showed they both had a wonderful trip, but were not inclined to settle in Australia. Every time Mum saw the pilot from the pilot ship jump onto the gangway her first thought was, 'I wonder if he has any post for us.' Dad decided they needed more air and a clearer view so he opened a cabin window and cleaned it. The steward soon shut it. There were notices all over the ship saying not to open windows as it interfered with air-conditioning.

With the sweltering heat, Dad decided that he needed shorts — which he had never worn in his life. Mum tried to find some at the shop, but no luck. Later that day whilst Mum was resting, Dad called out to her to bring her camera quick and take his photo. He had been sunbathing on deck and there he was, his skin looking red, wearing

Enjoying Australia.

nothing but his underpants. She felt so sick and ashamed, not sure how she could face anyone again. Not exactly a fine figure of a man. They did eventually buy shorts and Mum adjusted them to fit. On fancy dress night Mum and a new shipmate helped Dad to dress up with his camera equipment as 'Dickey Bird - smile please' He won first prize. He and Mum got lots of congratulations; he really enjoyed all the fun on board, a real change for both of them. Dad's prize — ha ha — was a souvenir ashtray. He managed to change it for a calendar.

They arrived in Sydney on May 3, and whilst still on deck could see John and Alwyn, Philip and Mary and grandchildren Beverley, Michelle and Melanie with them. Mum did sewing between touring. She re-covered their chairs and suite and made dresses for the children.

Dad helped Philip by doing some accountancy work in the office at Philip's company. Philip had set up Hockney Engineering and Welding Company in 1967 to manufacture bitumen sprayers, pumping sets, tippers and specialised transport equipment. He was hoping to eventually build petroleum tankers. Mum made a note of his certificates on the office wall.

Institute of Engineers and Designers.
Institute of Road Transport Engineers.
Certificate of Transportation of Propriety Co Hewco Pty, ltd 7-12-1967

John and Alwyn were in the process of moving into a rented furnished house in Parramatta. They had joined a singing group and were hoping they may have success with singing.

Mum and Dad had enjoyed catching up with the Australian family. They arrived back in England in September.

13 Deafness in the NHS

Back in cold, dark England I got a job as a midwife where I trained at St Luke's in Bradford; but I was in for a shock: I couldn't hear patients if I was standing at the end of their bed. There were echoes and whirring sounds, but voices were very difficult to understand. In offices or even in labour ward, right next to the patient, I was all right; but I felt that I might need to change career. In January I bought a correspondence course to study for more GCE 'O' levels to add to the three I already had. Most employers were asking for at least five. Six months later I had dropped the geography, Latin, British economic history, and physics — which were far too demanding to learn in a hurry — and passed the exams in human biology and French. By then I was adapting to not hearing by getting closer to patients before I spoke. Dad recommended a portable amplifier gadget that attached to telephones. I was learning to conceal the deafness, but was not really happy working in hospital where I might miss hearing something important.

Pauline, now married, was working as a District Nurse in Bedfordshire. We wondered whether I could cope better with that sort of work. There was a job for a District Nurse Midwife advertised in the next county in Hitchin, Hertfordshire. I applied for it and in the middle of December, 1970, on a cold foggy day, I went for an interview. I didn't really expect a reply between Christmas and the New Year, but I got a phone-call telling me that they were waiting for the doctor's report on hearing and asked had I already resigned?

I said, 'Yes, but I can withhold the resignation and work on a weekly basis until formalities are complete.' No need to do that, as your letter of appointment is to be written, but may be delayed with Christmas post. It was confirmed in slow clear speech on both ends of the phone that I should start work on January 4, 1971. On the strength of that call, I drove in awful foggy, snowy weather to Hitchin and reported in the office at 9.30 am.

I will change the name of the Nursing Officer to Miss Short. She was busy and I was asked to wait in a secretary's office. Miss Short arrived at 9.45 am and briefly introduced herself, then was busy on the phone for an hour before she finally called me to her office.

'I was not expecting you,' she said, 'The report on your hearing was not good.'

I suggested that I went to stay with my friend Pauline to await the official letter of refusal or appointment. She told me to wait outside whilst she made enquiries. No doubt she phoned various officials about my unexpected arrival. Finally she called me back saying, Yes, I was to be appointed. I would have much preferred to wait until matters were completed; but Miss Short was now insisting that I stayed. If I didn't, I might have trouble getting a job elsewhere because of the hearing, she said.

About 12.30 pm I drove four miles to the nurses' house at Letchworth, following Miss Short in her car. I lost her in the fog. After finding what I hoped was the address in the phone book in a red telephone box, I arrived. The empty house was freezing cold although Miss Short had phoned from the office to turn on the water and electricity. After doing the inventory, she left about 2 pm saying she would try to get pillows and blankets for the bed. I phoned to order coal for the fire and registered with the gas and electric companies. I had sent my luggage by goods train and it was at the station, but I had no time to collect it. So I bought some cheap sheets to start with and two bags of carry-away coal till the coal man delivered. Miss Short phoned at 5 pm, there were no blankets or pillows but she had arranged for me to stay the night with the nurse at Baldock. Also she had arranged that I meet the District Nurse in Hitchin next morning to be shown round the area.

I drove two miles through dark fog on icy roads to find the nurse at Baldock who was most kind and made me comfortable. After breakfast with her, I went back to Letchworth to light the fire and hopefully warm up the house. Then I met the Hitchin nurse who was very pleasant and I did the morning's visits with her. She took me to the office to collect my uniform and nursing bags and I drove back to Letchworth, stoked up the fire, went to collect my luggage from the station and bought a bit of food.

Mid-afternoon, Miss Short arrived with pillows and blankets and a radiator without a plug. She measured up for curtains at the scantily-netted cold windows; her manner was quite pleasant until she told me that I was being given a chance, but would have to see how I managed. We can't let the service down by you not hearing the phone. I was hearing everything she said and had already made lots of phone calls.

She also said that hearing would not be so important if I did factory nursing.

Although I had got well-started with unpacking, I again suggested that I went away until the formal letter arrived. Miss Short insisted that the letter was written and that I should stay and have a try.

Feeling very insecure after Miss S left, I had to force myself to get positive. I bought a plug for the radiator and some light bulbs, fixed them all up and made the bed. I got another plug for the naked wires on the Hoover and cleaned around. I was tired out; what with the snow, fog and weirdness, I felt as though I was getting a cold, so had an early night.

Next morning, I called in the office at 9 am to check on anything to be done. Miss Short showed her amazement that I wasn't working with the Hitchin nurse and demonstrated her annoyance verbally, repeating the fact that I wasn't expected, so couldn't expect things to be arranged. I was upset by this outburst, so Miss Short offered me a form to fill in, stating my 'notification to practice as a midwife'. She told me it should be her who was upset by all the extra work I was causing her. I returned the form and gave a verbal notification of my intention to leave just as soon as I could pack. I documented the whole event in my notebook.

I went to stay with Pauline and Colin. They were appalled and encouraged me to contact County Hall in Hertfordshire to see whether I was ever really expected. It turned out that, Yes, I had been appointed. They were most apologetic for the unwelcome time I had endured. I received a week's pay and all travelling expenses; but it had been a nasty experience and I was fully ready to leave nursing altogether. Pauline insisted that I would be fine on District and she contacted Miss Frost, the chief nursing officer in Bedfordshire. That resulted in my having an interview with the Chief Medical Officer and Miss Frost. I was offered a job and assured that if there were any problems I should discuss them; I was offered an electronic stethoscope to help with hearing blood pressures and foetal hearts. What a difference.

It was a relief to be on District. The hearing was scarcely a problem. Hearing aids were improving and I could hear my colleagues and the patients. There was a nice two bed-roomed house at Keysoe, a rural village nine miles north of Bedford, that went with the job. All was well with me again and I continued working in Bedfordshire for more than twelve years.

I was a District Nurse Midwife in Keysoe amongst a friendly group of colleagues. We worked six days a week and relieved each other on days-off. There was good continuity of care for midwifery patients whom we would know from antenatal until fourteen days after delivery. Some weeks we might be up all night or even two nights, working with mothers in labour and still have to do the day's work, sometimes driving up to a hundred miles a day around the rural villages of North Bedfordshire. There was no overtime or unsocial working-hours payments. It was just the way the job was organised. We might then have a quiet week and catch up on lost sleep.

Before I moved from Bradford, Mum had not been so well. Within two weeks of her first visit to doctor in August 1970, she was admitted to the private wing of the Bradford Royal Infirmary and had major surgery to remove part of her bowel. David was successfully selling pictures and was busy working on the Olympic poster for Munich. He financed the private care for Mum, which she thoroughly appreciated.

She had lots of friends and relatives visiting and supporting her, and made an excellent recovery. Dad bought their first colour television as a welcome home gift. He even cancelled some of his meetings to make sure that his wife came first.

During 1972 Dad had problems with his unstable diabetes. He was not the easiest of patients and Mum tried her best to help him keep to his diet; but he would go off to town for hours at a time, returning late for meals. He wore a name and address label on his wrist, which at least enabled strangers to help him safely home if he was found in confused or semi stupor-states. In July he was admitted to St Luke's with a possible stroke, but it was the diabetes problem. He was in for three weeks, became very bored and wanted fresh air. He got Mum to bring him papers and important paraphernalia, which he spread out over two lockers so that he could keep himself occupied.

He took photos of the nurses and when he was discharged and visited by his own GP, Dr Keith Manchester, took a photo of him too. Life at home was not easy. He could be in a stupor in the morning. Mum, who was finding looking after Dad very tiresome, worked out when to give him sugar, tea or breakfast. She had to help him eat and drink. But as soon as he felt better he could become cantankerous. She confides in her diary:

He would rave and shout about anything, wallpaper, TV programmes —
tries to phone them. Took too much blood when in hospital for tests,

aggressive and persistent. No efforts of mine are any use to him until he is helpless, I believe he stayed up all night, came to bed 6am, must have fallen asleep in chair which I found wet this morning and trousers soaked. Wobbly this morning — took him a full ten minutes to fill his syringe, but he refused help.

I suggested that Mum and Dad, along with Mum's friend Mary, should have a short holiday with me in Keysoe. They liked the idea, and came after visiting David in London. He had started making sketches and taking photographs for a double portrait he wanted to paint called My Parents. He did sketches of them both whilst visiting Dad in hospital and Mum at home: then in August he asked them to go to London for a few days so he could work more on the picture. Mary went with them. It turned out to be a family gathering. Paul, Jean and their children were in transit from a holiday in the Isle of Wight, and were staying in a friend's flat. They all had a meal round David's big dining table and enjoyed the next day sight-seeing together. By the time Mum sat for David to paint her she was feeling tired and wondering if David would find the task difficult. He was already finding the picture difficult and took several years before he was happy with it. There was a version with Mum in a black-and-white spotted silk dress and Dad sitting in profile view and doing nothing.

At the end of their stay with David in August, 1972, he drove them to visit me in Keysoe. He stayed for a meal and then returned to London. Mum, Dad and Mary spent three enjoyable days with me. Mum's friend Mary made coping with Mum and Dad together much easier for me. I was spared having to listen to Mum's complaints about her husband. My house was one of many on Keysoe Row. All detached, some old, some new. Dad found the place too isolated because you couldn't even walk to the nearest shop. They were intrigued with the little thatched roof Baptist church across the road from my house. There was a thatched caretaker's house attached to the church. In the churchyard, the man who built the church two hundred years ago had on his tombstone that he was the 'sole proprietor'.

In 1974 there was a major reorganisation of the National Health Service. I was currently employed with Bedfordshire County Council and accountable to the Chief Nursing Officer and two Nursing Officers under her. The county councils and local authority would no longer hold the finance and management of community health services.

The NHS Reorganisation 1948–1974

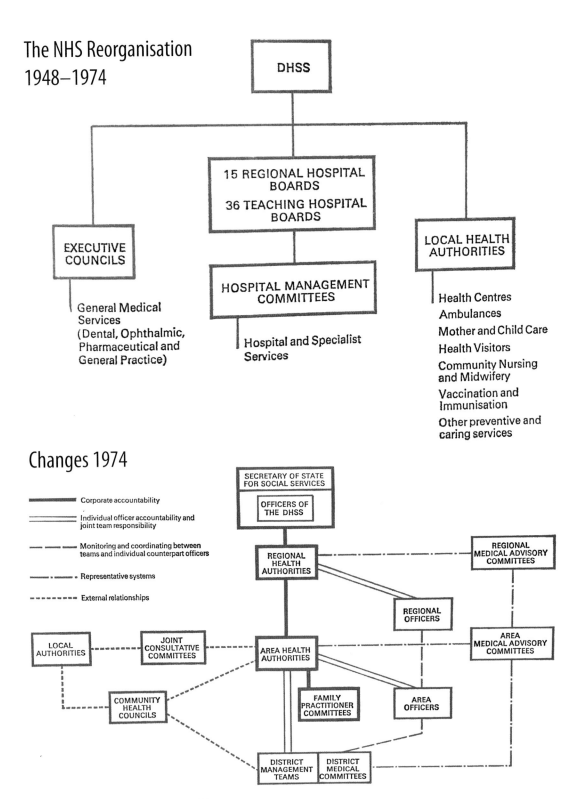

Buggering up the NHS in 1974: bigger management.

Likewise, Hospital Management committees would no longer finance hospital services. This was changed to a hierarchical management structure, with all health and administrative disciplines on each level of the Department of Health and Social Services. For nursing there was a Regional Nursing Officer; under her were Area Nursing Officers; then Divisional Nursing officers and several lower rank Nursing Officers. Those of us on the patient contact level saw it as 'too many chiefs and not enough Indians'.

We were working in geographical locations so we would serve villages, hamlets and become known in our areas as District Nurse Midwives. We delivered all babies at home unless an emergency transpired. Reorganisation changed this. Now we were allocated to General Practitioners' group practices as part of Primary Care Teams. Also beds were allocated in hospital maternity wards for GPs and district midwives to deliver normal confinements, taking the patient into hospital and home again. There was integration of hospital and community services on all levels of authority. GPs remained independent contractors. I was not happy about being a District Midwife in hospital and of course it raised the problem of not hearing from the hospital bed. So I left midwifery and continued as a District Nurse attached to a group of doctors. The doctors had their own practice nurses. As District Nurses we would visit doctors as necessary to discuss patients. We had already been doing that with the old method, but this was the new official regime.

There were changes in pay and conditions. I had a slight pay increase from an annual salary of £1,644 to £1,890 — about £13,770 in 2016. There were payments for overtime and for unsocial hours. We were quickly informed that there was no need for everyone to work at weekends and that we must take hours off in lieu of over-time. Along with these changes, I moved house to Bromham, a lovely village and closer to Bedford town centre.

Just before reorganisation there was an invitation for hospital and community nursing staff to take a course for the London University Diploma in Nursing. Studying seemed a good idea and I joined a colleague called Maggie to do the course. We were warned at the start that it was a pilot scheme; exam standards would be very high, so none of us were expected to pass. Well if that doesn't motivate you, I don't know what does. There were weekly lectures to attend and test papers to submit. We were a mixed class, about twenty-two of us, mostly senior hospital staff and tutors. I had trouble hearing the lectures, but Maggie loaned me her notes and we studied together as we walked our dogs round the park. I also bought books on the topics. The course stimulated ideas and new ways of thinking. About half the contenders passed, including Maggie and me.

One of the tutors and I were the only two to pass with a distinction. Success made me feel more worthwhile. Also, keeping up with knowledge by reading reports and advances in nursing would compensate for my deafness. I even managed to become a Practical Work Teacher of Student District Nurses, which involved taking them round the District to teach them the practical skills of organising their work-load and carrying out the nursing techniques and care of patients.

14 The Seventies

I believe there is a time for everything. The time for taking the Diploma in Nursing was right for me personally although it did me no good professionally. I applied for many management posts, but deafness became a major block. I had to accept that I would remain a District Nurse in the Bedford area for the rest of my nursing career.

Two subjects, the cause and effect of disease and psychology, filled me with enthusiasm to learn more. Many of my fellow learners smirked that psychology was just common-sense. Well if that was so, then common-sense was a rare commodity as far as I could see. Psychology offered marvellous ideas about tolerance, communication, attitudes and in fact the mental state and how it connected with the physical. Apart from congenital problems, the cause of disease was mainly attributable to a breakdown of the immune system. I preferred to use the word homeostasis where the body maintains normality despite daily variations in diet, exercise, travel, climate and abuse. Attitudes,

Celebrating David's book launch, 1976
Back row: David, me, John
Front row: Philip, Dad, Mum, Paul.
Photo by Telegraph & Argus.

thought and emotions were involved. The mental and the physical were not separate in the cause and effect of disease. I recalled those poor malnourished children in Africa — the state of them on admission and the reason that had happened. Ignorance without knowledge was a major factor. My own breakdown, lack of appetite, loss of weight, nervous agitation, twitching, depression, was an example of this. I sensed there was an imbalance; but now I could see things clearer because I understood how the energy of emotions and relationships could result in such serious illness. Patients weren't the only people that I was observing.

My parents were suffering from the effects of disease. Mum had severe rheumatic pains in her hands, wrists and feet. There were times when her whole body would cry out in pain and unhappiness. She wanted gentle love and companionship with Dad, regular mealtimes, homely chats, sharing their pride of successful children. She compensated by visiting lots of people at their homes, or in hospital if she heard they were sick. Although she would constantly complain that Dad wasted his money, she would buy new dresses, coats, shoes or hats. Not in excess, but enough to keep her well-dressed and always looking tidy. She would be very suitably dressed for chapel. I don't recall ever seeing her wear trousers; but she did buy nice clothes, especially when her hands were too painful to sew her own. Fairly frequently she would release her frustrations with Dad by weeping and usually felt better for the tears. Her biggest pleasures in life were family, the five of us, and her grandchildren. Only two of my brothers had children at that time, although later John married Helen and had a stepdaughter; Paul was near enough for Mum to babysit and, as the children grew, they would visit her. Although Philip was in Australia, Mum and Dad accepted his invitation to visit them for two long holidays. She constantly craved that Dad would be more aware of her and show gratitude for the diabetic meals she served. Often he wouldn't even clear space on the dining table to put the meals on, far too busy making posters or writing letters.

The effect of Dad's imbalance and disease was diabetes. During my nursing observations I had seen that some diabetic patients were organised with well-structured lives. Some would write detailed diaries. Others with a hand-ruled notebook might add a column describing the weather day by day along with the dose of insulin, urine, blood test and appointment with the doctor. Dad was far too busy for such daily trivia. He would be working from morn till night. Mum thought he was working on nothing useful, but who knows the value

of another's work? He truly never stopped until his body could take no more and his mind would sometimes become full of anger or con-fusion. He would criticise people, complain about a newspaper article or be furious that Mum had moved something that was important. Sometimes he would want sex and rushed to the library or bookshop to get books on the subject to show Mum — and disgust her.

Sugar imbalance was the cause, affecting him both physically and mentally. He would become unsteady or ravenously hungry, or dopey, or sick but kept assuring Mum that he was fine and didn't want a doctor. She would give him sugar, or a meal, or check he had his insulin, lest he collapse into semi-consciousness and had to be admitted to hospital. Even in hospital he would complain and want to get home, too busy to stay there. Then he would gradually stabilise and be charming and grateful to the doctors and nurses. Mum was certainly fighting a losing battle with Dad. When he was good and in balance he would go to Eastbrook chapel with her, and they joined Mum's sisters and a group of elderly from Eastbrook on Methodist holidays. Mum would worry about him raving or getting aggressive, and upset herself even before they set off. This could affect her bowel, which became irritable.

I had already made a comment that I regretted soon after I moved to Bedford. Mum had phoned me many times to complain about Dad, saying that no-one understood what he was like. They were living separate lives, but she cooked his meals and he was never grateful for anything. She would continue when I visited home, saying how difficult her life was. On this particular evening they were on holiday in Kes-wick. She phoned to tell me how he was ruining the holiday for her and everyone else. I enquired whether she had ever thought of divorc-ing him. She was horrified at such a suggestion and made me feel the size of a mouse. I wanted to creep away, hardly believing what I had said. I dreaded my next visit when I would have to face her. When I did, Mum just said, 'I don't understand what you meant'. There was not much discussion. Mum was 'always right': not much point arguing and nothing really to discuss at that time. We just cut the words by playing Scrabble, which was a very regular thing to do when I came home — either Scrabble or reading the paper. The paper could last forever by reading births, deaths, marriages and all the classified adverts as well as the news and crosswords.

After she died and I saw her diaries, I noticed that John had made the same suggestion back in 1961, before Dad had diabetes. He said: 'Why don't you leave him?' Mum replied: 'for better or worse'. To her diary she confided that she was nearly at the end of her tether. How heavenly indeed it must be to live with people in peace.

I still found it very difficult being alone with her. She had a powerful energy that needed diluting with more people. Most of the time she no longer bothered me, but even the thought of being alone with her made me plan a hasty return to work. However I did need to have some sort of talk about Dad and his changing personality. I tried to explain that he wasn't really responsible for his awful state of mind when he was raving and being aggressive: it was the sugar imbalance. Of course I had to agree that he should try to be punctual for mealtimes, not wandering round town carrying heavy bags of gear and being late for meals. Sadly, I told her that it was unlikely he would change. The only hope would be for her to change her attitude and accept that Dad was quite a sick man, who would not change his habits to become the loving partner she kept praying for. I assured her that she was doing incredibly well at caring for him, sometimes having to feed him on the floor whilst he recovered from semi-coma; other times keeping her cool when she felt like exploding. She was brilliant at offering him the right food. It was no fault of hers if he was late to eat it.

I think she told herself that I did understand her problem, but she was also aware that I could not offer the companionship she craved. I didn't like to tell her that all of my life I had heard her complain about Dad. I had wondered whether the constant complaining to him and about him since the war years, along with his deafness, had been a major trigger in his homeostatic imbalance. I had also been aware for years, that Mum's rheumatic pain was worse after arguments with Dad in the days during the war and since.

Despite everything there were memorable and happy events during the 1970s. Their constant money problems were resolved by David, who arranged a monthly allowance for each of them to cover their pleasures as well as their needs. Whilst Dad was in hospital David told Mum to stop chasing after buses and start using taxis, so she no longer had to rely on Paul for lifts. However, Paul remained stalwart at supporting her and transporting her to hospitals and other places whenever he could. The first taxi was shared with her sisters Jane and Rebe and Dad's sister Audrey. They were going to see Dad in hospital.

The rain was pouring as they left, so Mum ordered a taxi which took the others home and then her. The fare cost £1 — about £10 in 2016 — which seemed terribly extravagant but worth it.

David was on Desert Island discs in 1972. He told presenter Roy Plomley that the book he would take was out-of-print, called Route 99, by Floyd Carter. He said it was a pornographic book full of spelling mistakes written by a little man in an office. Mum wrote in her diary: was he joking or just one of his cheerfully disrespectful idioms? David had never hidden his sexuality and in May, 1961, Bradford's *Telegraph & Argus* newspaper had published a story that David had won a prize of £25 for the best of three hundred entries in a competition or an exhibition. The picture was called *The Most Beautiful Boy in the World* and alluded to a fellow male student on whom David had a crush. Mum wrote: I wonder who he is — self-portrait? Or contemporary?

David was having many exhibitions and was in the news a lot, mostly good reports; but Mum and Dad had a shock when Jack Hazan's *The Bigger Splash* documentary film was reviewed. Both, in their separate ways, found out more about homosexuality through booklets and books and scarcely at all by talking together.

When the film arrived in Bradford in 1975 Mum told Dad she was going to see it with a friend. Dad declined her invitation to join them. Mum left his meal ready and off she went. They arrived early and were having a snack in the foyer when Mum suddenly saw Dad outside. She asked: 'Oh are you coming in?' He said: 'Er no, I have a few places to visit'. The film had just started when Mum saw Dad walk in and sit a few rows in front of her. He left hurriedly as soon as it ended. When Mum arrived home, Dad asked: 'How was it?' She said: 'Well what did you think of it?' He was taken aback, didn't know she had seen him. She told her diary:

How silly — afraid our minds are not in tune at all. Why should we not be frank and open? To me, the film was a revelation — suppose I am a very slow learner, and because of my upbringing — puritanical. I am eager to learn and to broaden my mind according to the times, without lowering my standards and principles, but Ken is always hot tempered and aggressive. He is blaming David's friends.

David was her darling boy, she tried to protect him from this sort of publicity, but had to accept that there was a limit to what she could say and do; besides, films and articles about David's homosexuality didn't seem to worry him. Although homosexuality was not much spoken of, I had first encountered it in 1953. There were several male nurses who were called 'queer'. They were popular friendly nurses, usually with a great sense of humour. There was also whispering that some of the Ward Sisters were lesbians. There was no big issue about any of them, merely another fact of life.

In 1974 David got the first of many honorary degrees conferred on him, this one at Leeds University, from the Duchess of Kent.

There was a spell in June, 1976, when Mum was in Bradford Royal Infirmary having a foot operation, and Dad was in St Luke's Hospital with diabetes followed by a prostate problem. They wrote letters to each other! Later in 1976, when David's first volume of autobiography was published, *David Hockney* by David Hockney, we had a full family gathering at the Devonshire Arms, Bolton Abbey. Philip and John made a special visit from Australia; the local press took a family photo of us all.

Looking a bit raffish in his highwayman's hat, Paul doing a great job as Lord Mayor of Bradford 1977.

Paul became Lord Mayor of Bradford on May 24 1977, the day before his forty-sixth birthday, during the Queen's Silver Jubilee year. That was a proud time for us all and an absolute joy to Mum and Dad. Paul proved to be a pocket dynamo and his charity raised many thousands of pounds for a children's outward bound centre at Ilkley. A few years later, a new road in Bradford was named after him — Hockney Road.

David had been several years working on his double portrait, *My Parents*. They would be a difficult subject, so I was not surprised when Mum told me in early August, 1976, that David had phoned her to say he had decided to scrap the painting. Mum was naturally upset but had to respect his decision.

Hayward Gallery: Mum, Dad and David in front of the painting. His double-portrait of them.

Dad was furious and phoned David to tell him so. A short while later Dad repented and phoned David again. He said; 'David, disregard what I have just said. I am sorry.' A few days later David phoned. Mum wrote in her diary:

Started again on portrait. I ask what changed his mind? What influence? He says he had new inspiration. Anyway in a few days he is going to New York so he will be able to collect himself. I only want him to be happy and satisfied with his work. Nothing less will do!

He completed the portrait *My Parents,* it was first shown at the Hayward Gallery in July, 1977.

Dad was most surprised and honoured to see that David had hung a picture of Bertrand Russell among his exhibition pictures. Dad drew it in the 1950s during the Campaign for Nuclear Disarmament marches. David felt it was good enough to show.

In March, 1978, Mum and Dad had another trip to Australia, staying with the family. Throughout the 1970s they had holidays with Eastbrook

Dad's picture of Bertrand Russell exhibited in London by David.

Chapel members, with John and David at Portmeirion in Wales, in
London with David and several times with me in Bedford. They did a
coach tour of Europe, and stayed two nights at Glyndebourne when
Pauline and I went with them to the dress rehearsal of *The Magic Flute*.
David had produced the sets, which were wonderful and well-received
by the audience and press.

Dad was going to evening classes for photography, etching and
silkscreen printing. Mum went to several classes and groups, and
joined an educational scheme to help her teach illiterate adult students
to read.

By 1978 there had been several management changes in District
Nursing, with an increasing number of meetings with Nursing Officers.
I did not like sitting round those large conference tables because of my
hearing. I could not hear the Nursing Officers unless I was facing them.
Although I was renting a lovely Nurses' house in Bromham that went
with the job, I decided that I needed to have my own house. If or when
I had to retire because of deafness, I would not be restricted to a

council flat. I had a little money saved from Zambia, so did a house

search and finally decided on an end-terrace house opposite Bedford
Park. It had three bedrooms and an upstairs bathroom, plus a downstairs shower-room. I needed a mortgage, but there were problems with
that because having two bathrooms was a gateway to multiple
occupation according to the building society. My plan was to accommodate my hobbies of books, photography, cooking and sewing. Philip
was around at the time. He kindly arranged a family loan that enabled
me to buy the house and pay back when I could. I was very grateful to
my brothers for their help to make me secure and independent in my
chosen house.

I moved in on December 6, 1978, and invited Mum and Dad, plus
Pauline and Colin and their two young boys to join me for Christmas
dinner.

I took photos of Dad walking in Bedford Park wearing his
fluorescent armbands, Russian-style hat and coat full of extra pockets.
This would be the last time I saw him alive.

On February 7, 1979, Paul accompanied Mum and Dad on the train
to London where David had invited them for a luxurious one-night

Dad in his Russian hat. My last photo of him. December 25, 1978.

stay at the Savoy Hotel. Mum was not all that well and struggled as Paul took her to join Dad at Kasmin's art gallery, where David had a new exhibition. They had tea at Fortnum and Masons; saw the pantomime *Aladdin* at the Palladium and met Wayne Sleep, Danny La Rue and Ken Tyler, a printer friend of David's from New York. After breakfast in the Savoy dining room, they took the train back home to Bradford. Mum still did not feel well and saw doctor about her neck and head pains.

Memorable as the Winter of Discontent for political reasons and public service strikes, 1979 was also the coldest winter since the big freeze of 1962–63. Bradford was icy-cold and snow was forecast. Dad really enjoyed his visit to London and told everyone he met how well he was and what a good trip they had. On the Friday he was in town in the very cold weather. When he got home, Mum thought he looked quite ill. Sure enough he was up and down and very sick during the night. He was sick all day and by Saturday night was no better. Snow was falling heavily and the ambulance men were on strike. On Sunday she called the emergency doctor, but what with ambulance strike and snow falling fast and settling, Dad could not be taken to hospital. He seemed a little better that night, no more sickness, but he was not eating. On Monday, Doctor Manchester visited and asked to be kept informed. The ambulance strike would be over later that day.

The snow was non-stop and blizzards set in. Mum, who kept changing sheets to keep Dad comfortable, managed to get a urine test that was highly positive for sugar. Ice had formed in the night and more snow was falling. Paul drove to see Mum and Dad saying the roads were treacherous. Doctor Manchester phoned mid-morning on Tuesday to say he had got Dad a bed in hospital and the ambulance was on its way. It took an hour with lights flashing and struggling through the snow for the ambulance to arrive. Mum did not feel well enough to go with Dad, as she normally would have done. The ambulance men didn't advise it anyway. Paul managed to drive Mum to hospital later. To her delight Dad was sitting up in bed asking how they all were managing in the snow. He said he had enjoyed a snack.

On Wednesday, Mum was still feeling poorly herself but got things ready to take to Dad. It snowed all day and at 5 pm Dad phoned her from the hospital and said not to visit because the weather was too bad. He said, 'Things can be brought tomorrow.' Mum was a bit sad but relieved to be able to get to bed, knowing Dad was being cared for. By

Thursday the snow was even worse: terrible blizzards made even some main roads impassable, buses were stopped. Paul phoned to say he was stranded in Bradford. Mum rang the hospital. A nurse said there were many phone calls from people who could not get there, she could not get home herself. Dad phoned Paul later to ask how Mum was and that he had been up and walking about.

At 7 am on Friday, February 16, Paul phoned Mum to tell her that the hospital just called him to say Dad was on the danger list. Mum started to get dressed. Paul would get over to pick her up, driving through the snow as quickly as he could. He arrived at 8.30am. Mum had things ready to take for Dad. 'Don't bother Mum, he's gone,' Paul said. Dad had had a heart-attack and died.

Paul had to tell us all. It was a massive shock. We had become so accustomed to Dad going in and out of hospital. I had to agree with Mum when she said she could not imagine Ken doing nothing and wondered what he would be given to do in the place prepared for him. 'Although I have seen him change over many months — he never gave in, and battled on, just being in a world of his own,' she said. The funeral service was at Eastbrook Hall in a small chapel. It was the actual room in which Ken used to teach his Sunday School scholars.

A month later on March 16, Philip's oldest daughter Beverley was to get married. Philip had invited me over to Australia. Auntie Jane, Mum's only remaining sister, was also going. Hasty plans were made for Mum to go for the wedding, have a short stay in Australia, then fly directly to America to spend time with David. So that was how Laura started her life without Kenneth. Mum spent a month in Australia before flying to Los Angeles for a week.

From her diary account she did a good bit of partying in California, making notes of names so she could remember all the people who were introduced and so kind to her. The first day on 12 April, David took her to visit a friend of his, Michael Caine, saying he was a film director and an actor, Cockney born, with his wife Shakira and their little girl Natasha. They had only arrived in California a few months ago and had a beautiful modern American home. Another of David's neighbours threw a long-running party where Mum met Marty Stevens, Rachel Roberts, Peter Langhan, Rock Hudson, Rupert Allan who had just come from Australia and was to interview Barry Norman of BBC TV and Neil Hartley, who was English and worked with Tony Richardson, the Oscar-winning film director of *Tom Jones* and *The*

Charge of the Light Brigade, who came from Shipley in Bradford. I was surprised to read in her diary that she managed with her arthritic hands to use chopsticks at a Japanese restaurant. Vincent Price and Coral Brown became her friends. She was driven to Farmers Market, Huntington Museum, Gemini Printers, Disneyland, Hollywood, Sunset Boulevard — all in seven days. David flew back home with her on April 19, 1979.

I went back to Eccleshill to stay for a while at Hutton Terrace, clearing the attics and cellar, giving a really good clean as the rubbish was moved out.

15 Another Ken

In the summer of 1978, when I was looking for a suitable house to buy, I went to a leaving party for a colleague. They were fairly regular events and alcohol was flowing freely. Although booze never suited me, I had drunk a few glasses that made me sleepy. The evening was warm and balmy and we were outside amongst the tree-edged grassy lawn. I settled my head comfortably on a tree trunk and slumbered.

Ken Wathey, a male District Nurse, was sitting on a bench close by. Eventually as I woke up, he greeted me. Seeing me the worse for drink pleased him, he thought I was of his ilk — which I soon discovered was dipsomania. Turned out that we both were born in Yorkshire; his sister lived in my hometown of Bradford.

Under the new rules of the NHS, District Nurses were allowed to buy lunch in the hospital dining room. I had seen Ken there occasionally but not really taken much notice of him. As we began to be friendly, I discovered he had a hilarious sense of humour. Whoever sat on his table would get large doses of laughter with their meals.

Born in 1926, Ken had a great love and knowledge of art, artists, and art galleries. When he left school he worked as an apprentice graphic artist, but was called up to do National Service. He went down a coal mine as a Bevin Boy, then when he hurt his back in the pit was transferred to the Army, first in the catering corps, then in the medics. He was stationed at Millbank Barracks, a stone's throw from the Tate Gallery in London. He got to know all the pictures in the Tate and visited all other London galleries. When he left the army he did nurse training, first mental nursing, then general, and finally district nursing.

As District Nurses we worked ten days then had four days off. Ken and I started to go regularly to London where he exhibited his knowledge of art and the Metropolis. Sometimes we would picnic in the countryside or maybe at Woburn Abbey, where Ken would paint in the open air. One of his favourite projects was copying paintings that he loved. He would buy a postcard or catalogue from the gallery shop and could take weeks to complete a copy of a Matisse, Cezanne, Van Gogh or maybe Picasso. If not a copy he would paint in the style of artists he admired. He was an avid reader of several library books a week, many of them biographies of artists. He had a nurse's council flat quite near the new house that I was buying. His sitting room had a

permanent easel in place usually supporting a work in progress. He was also an avid imbiber and was a regular visitor to the local pub. London and picnics often had to be cancelled because Ken would have a headache and needed to stay the day in bed until he sobered up and was ready to work. When he first visited my house I offered him a sherry and poured it into one of my rather small sherry glasses. He guffawed at the sight of it, called them medicine glasses and filled himself a whole tumbler full of my Bristol Cream, which would normally last me from one Christmas to the next.

Keen to oblige, but not keen to finance a big supply of alcohol, I started making my own wine and sherry, which sort of worked; but maintaining supplies against demand was hard because Ken would be drinking from the syphon of the incompletely-matured Winchester bottles.

Despite his dipsomania, he was always a kind, reliable and popular nurse. We became good friends. We visited each other and shared home-cooked meals together. In fact he could hide the drink problem most of the time. He could talk on virtually any subject except sport, although his favourite topics were art and history. Sometimes I would go to the pub with him, but must admit that I found it boring. Not much of a drinker myself; the repetition and laughter about trivia from half-drunk friends would make me tired. When we first went to Cambridge for the day, there was a favourite pub of Ken's which he told me did marvellous lunches. I followed him to the place, but was appalled at his choice. There was a smell of grease, dirty net curtains at the windows, dark lighting, a sticky carpet to walk on, and sticky tables to eat from. He was a clean and well-dressed person, so must have been the worse for drink when he last ate there. I put up with it the first time we went, can't recall what we ate but never went again. I told him after we left; he scarcely believed me until the next visit to Cambridge, when he opened his eyes and nose to the place and agreed with me that it was awful.

When I moved house I invited him to meet Mum and Dad on Christmas Day. He already knew Pauline and Colin. The thought of having a non-alcoholic Christmas with my teetotal parents was not his idea of celebrating, so he declined the invitation in favour of having dinner at his local pub. When Dad died two months later, Ken was

Ken Wathey 1979: a dapper, charming, artistic and funny man, but troubled.

sorry that he didn't accept my Christmas invitation. He would love to have met the other Ken.

Within the year after Dad died, Ken met Mum and all the rest of my family and I met his two sisters and his nephews. We had both been single all our lives, enjoyed our independence and were not particularly looking for romance. We were quite happy as things were. We took a holiday in Venice, where Ken showed off his knowledge of cuisine. From the menu, he recommended lobster thermidor. The *maître d'* showed us a choice of lobsters and Ken affirmed which one would be fine. I wondered what the weight scale had to do with anything, but I was being educated so sat down to await the meal. It was truly delicious, but we couldn't quite finish the generous portions. When the bill came Ken's face suddenly went as red as the lobster and he visibly shook. I thought he was having a stroke. As I was wondering how to resuscitate him, he pushed the bill to me. At first I couldn't understand the Italian writing, then I looked closer and saw it would cost our entire money that was budgeted for the whole week. When he read the menu, he thought the price was for the whole meal. It turned out it was cost 'per gram' by weight, so that is what those scales were for. We spent the rest of the happy week on take-out sandwiches or simply bread rolls.

Deafness finally obliged me to take early retirement in 1982 when I was forty-eight. The trigger was a meeting round the conference table, when the Divisional Nursing officer conducting the meeting specifically asked me something that I could not hear. Next morning she called me to her office and said I should see the Occupational Health Doctor with a view to retiring. What a weird consultation that was. There were two lights outside the doctor's room, one red and one green. The red light was wait, the green light meant enter. I sat watching the red light until it changed to green. I knocked on the door and tentatively opened it and walked into the room. The doctor had his back to me as he sat at his desk facing a window. There was a chair beside him, also facing the window. I slowly walked towards him, waiting for acknowledgement. At last he swung his chair round to face me and said, 'You are very deaf aren't you? Did you hear what I have been saying?' Well, my heart sank, I knew this was really the end. There was not much else to be said because I had heard nothing. I muttered that I could usually hear patients all right, and would partly lip-read when I was facing someone. Although I knew the end was coming, it was quite a shock to have such an interview. There had been no complaints from either colleagues or patients. Of course he reported to the hierarchy that I should take early retirement.

Meanwhile three colleagues, including Pauline and Maggie with whom I studied for the Diploma in Nursing, had asked me to join them on a 'biophysical medicine' acupuncture course, which would run for six weekends at monthly intervals. It did sound interesting, but was quite expensive and I knew that my lump-sum retirement superannuation would not be all that healthy. Nurses' pay was abysmally low at that time. I had no idea what road I would take when I left nursing.

Fortune favoured me during a trip home to Bradford with Ken. I had let Mum know I would soon be leaving nursing. Ken and I were visiting Paul and Jean and family for a meal. Ken mentioned the acupuncture course and Paul said, 'Why not do it?' 'Well,' I said, 'it might be a waste of money, and maybe I wouldn't be able to hear it.' Nothing much more was said, but as we were leaving Paul pushed an envelope into my hand. It contained a cheque for the first weekend's fees and a note — for your first weekend of the acupuncture course.

It was a marvellous course run by Chris and Ian, two modern-style acupuncturists who used electro acupuncture and auriculo-therapy, as well as more traditional methods. We were at a conference hotel in Watford. The course was well-structured with printed modules, lectures and practical work. My friends filled me in with what I didn't hear and loaned me their notes. After the first weekend I returned home with some basic equipment and needles that would enable me to relieve pain and help people stop smoking. I couldn't wait to test it. I had plenty of guinea pigs amongst my colleagues. Amazing to me, the treatment worked — for back aches, shoulder pain, hips and knees. Three friends came to stop smoking. I explained my new learning to them, how the tiny acupuncture needle would be left in a certain position in their ear and would take away the craving, probably by stimulating the release of endorphins in the brain. They would still have to overcome the habit of smoking and acknowledge the difference between habit and craving. Incredibly they stopped. That was just the boost I needed. This was my route to follow.

I didn't intend charging my early recruits: I was grateful for their confidence in me. But with so many positive results, they would offer me a few pounds toward the rest of my course. So I earned as I learned and completed the course. Getting good results with conditions such as hay fever, sinus and stress problems, was exciting. Out of the four of us, I was the only one who took the exams and passed them all. By then I was charging about £5 for a consultation/treatment, enabling me to buy more books to enhance my learning. Through books, I studied the Eastern origins of acupuncture, yin and yang and the five elements. I never mastered the twelve pulses, but I fully believed that energy was a vital factor in the homeostatic balance of life.

I subscribed to alternative medicine magazines and saw an advertisement for a course on iridology at Cambridge. It was close enough to drive from Bedford. The Cambridge course was for about twelve weekends over six months. The theory was that the colours and markings in the iris of the eye represented states of health, genetic inheritance and constitutional types. The practice was to print outlines of the eye, mapped out into parts of the body. These were laboriously filled in with coloured pencils, as we scrutinised each other's eyes with a torch and magnifying glass. There were a few expensive books on the subject, mostly American, although iridology was founded by an Hungarian physician. He noted how the iris of an injured owl changed as he nursed it to health. I don't think there was any conclusive evidence about the value of iridology, but sometimes things can work without such evidence. On completion of the course I gained my certificate and was on the Register of Iridologists. My plan was to do my own research as I continued with the acupuncture. I was taken aback when a gentleman phoned for an appointment and gave no clue as to his health needs. On the day he came, I felt rather like a fortune-teller with the iris as my crystal ball. In fact I felt a bit of a fraud. He looked perfectly normal as I invited him to sit comfortably and proceeded to colour my chart with his eye markings. On completion, I pointed out that the iris would merely guide me to certain weaknesses in his constitution or with a particular organ or system of his body.

I put the coloured charts in front of us both. I can't recall exactly what I told him, I merely explained as I interpreted the marks. Finally I asked him: 'Does that give you any sort of clue to your health and is there any particular issue of health that is worrying you?' His reply was: 'I couldn't have explained it better than you have just done.'

Was it beginner's luck, or was there something in it? My client was certainly delighted with his consultation. The trouble was I had nothing to offer in the way of treatment except acupuncture that he didn't particularly want. In fact he was happy to go on his way with the

coloured chart I gave him.

There was a back-up course at Cambridge on herbal medicines, but it was not a recognised official qualification. I looked around in my magazines and found an advertisement for a four-year course on Medical Herbalism. It was a combination of correspondence and annual seminars, plus three hundred hours of clinical training to be spent with practicing herbalists. I applied and got started. The course was very intensive. Subjects included botany, materia medica, pharmacology, nutrition, physiology, pathology, laboratory medical science, orthodox medicines, diagnosing, as well as ethics, pharmacy and legislation. There were annual exams to be passed and on completion almost a whole week of exams including practical history taking, consultation, diagnosing, prescribing, as well as written work. Student colleagues were always generous, sharing their notes with me to fill in the gaps when I couldn't hear.

Week after week I joined a herbal clinic at Balham in London for practical experience as well as a local herbalist to gain all my hours of witnessing herbalism. Ken supported me with my studies by having great confidence in my abilities and an interest in the subjects that I was learning. We continued to travel together, visiting my mother and his sister in Bradford.

He had a pharmacist friend in Bedford who had a chemist shop. One day as Ken was out on his rounds he wasn't feeling too well. He got a prescription from the doctor for septrin, a combination antibiotic and sulphonamide, used to prevent or treat chest or bladder infections. He asked his chemist friend to dispense the septrin and took the first dose with a drink of water. He then drove the half-mile to the hospital for lunch, parked his car and walked into the dining room. There were six of us on our usual table. It was my last week before retiring. Barbara, a nursing officer, was first to see Ken. She almost ran from the table to catch him and sit him on a chair; he was bright red and gasping for breath. A whole group of us rushed to help and lifted him into her car that was quickly driven round the block to casualty. He was in anaphylactic shock and was hastily given adrenalin and an intravenous drip. His whole body was bloated and covered in red blotches. He was wheezing and rolling his swollen tongue — a frightening event, both for him to endure and for us to witness. How lucky that he had driven himself to the hospital rather than home. He recovered and was discharged the next day.

One of my favourite herbs from the iridology course was fresh garlic, which had a wide range of anti-bacterial properties. Ken was determined to never have antibiotics again and was willing to try what I offered. I bought a bulb of garlic and chopped two cloves into small pieces and put them on a dessertspoon. Ken swallowed the whole spoonful with a glass of water. The taste was horrible and he gipped a bit, but garlic became his favourite medicine, because he found an extra side-effect: it raised his mood and would take away headaches, leaving him almost euphoric.

I finally finished district nursing. Acupuncture became the source of income for my learning fees and reference books. I could not officially practice herbalism until I became fully-qualified.

As Ken reached retirement age — sixty in those days — we planned to leave Bedford and live in Yorkshire again. We had spent a few days at Flamborough Head in a cottage that my brother Paul owned. The air was beautifully clean and fresh, so we decided to move to the East Yorkshire coast. Initially we were looking for a property each, but instead we found a large Victorian semi-detached house in Vernon Road, Bridlington, which already had an acupuncture clinic, strange as that may seem. There was ample room for Ken to have the second-floor with bedroom, bathroom and another bedroom to use as his studio. I still had two years of study to complete my four-year course of medical herbalism. The house was perfect, with two dry cellars for herb storage and the current clinic facilities to see patients.

Ken was sixty in August, 1986, and I still had a house to sell. We stayed in Bedford to continue working as I waited for the buyer to complete the sale of my house. We finally moved to Bridlington in November, 1986.

16 One Day at a Time

I had not realised how stressful Ken had found the two months of waiting to move; but within the first couple of weeks in Bridlington I saw that he was in a sorry state, drinking far too much, concerned that he would ruin my life. He thought he should move back to Bedford, where he could end his days with daily visits to his old friends at the pub. Life was difficult. Some days he never left his room, then he would go out and stock up on vodka, constantly saying he had made a mistake by moving. Sometimes there was verbal abuse and criticisms, but never physical abuse.

He was eating well and we shared walks with the dog and days out, but there would always be the cloud of needing alcohol. We had a few friends visit us from Bedford but before they came Ken would get panicky and start drinking. By the time they arrived his speech was slurry and tended to be crude and boring. Gradually I started putting people off to cover up the embarrassment. He didn't want visitors either and he registered with a doctor to get some 'antabuse' in order to treat himself and stop the dependence, but he didn't persist. He said he liked drinking.

Anxiety was accompanied by uncertainty and my deafness seemed to be getting worse. I advertised my new clinic, but was worrying whether Ken was inside or outside the waiting room area by the front door. I had never been offered disability help with my early retirement and decided to find out if any financial help was available. I registered with a doctor and asked his advice. His reply stunned me: 'Don't come to me with your ailing business. Deafness is not a disease.' That worked wonders. I didn't visit a doctor again for fifteen years. I studied hard and gradually increased my patients.

I talked with Ken, assuring him that I understood what a massive life change he had made. If he really felt he must go back, well so be it, but of course I desperately hoped that would not happen. I joined Al Anon, for friends and relatives of alcoholics, after seeing an advertisement in the local paper. Al Anon was a great help. I could see alcoholism as the disease it was. There were some terribly sad stories told at the meetings, especially where children and bailiffs were concerned. My problems became less as I went to those meetings. I accepted they were Ken's problems, his illness, his demons as he called them; all I could do was offer support and, of course, care in the way of meals and housekeeping.

A most worrying twenty-four hours occurred when, unbeknown to me, Ken joined a fisherman for the day on a fishing boat, returning late at night, drinking, stumbling and losing his way home. He slept on a bench near the harbour and woke up feeling dreadful. He finally arrived back armed with rum and vodka, likening himself to Captain Bligh. He disappeared into his bedroom for two days. Eventually he approached me with his suitcase packed and said he was moving back to Bedford. 'Well I can't stop you, although I'll be sorry to see you go,' I said. I knew not to argue or criticise. I suggested a meal first and maybe he could take a packed lunch. I was playing for time, feeling very upset and insecure.

He decided he would visit a drinking friend in Brighton before going to Bedford. He would come back in a few days for the rest of his luggage. We had a meal, I packed him food for the journey and off he went. I had no idea whether he would return. Five days later he came back to talk. He was fed up with the demon drink, had spent all his money on his drinking friend and decided to try going to Alcoholics Anonymous. It was a difficult time. Together we discussed the twenty-four hour AA book and the daily readings, wondering about the 'power greater than me' — which was most convenient to call God. We talked of religion and church, how it was a great social club where congregations could have a good sing and a chat. But church was not the answer for us. Ken wrote in his diary during March 1988:

I am negative and ill at ease with myself. I do hope these silly moods will pass soon — I can't think why Margaret puts up with it — not much fun for her — I feel so weary and yet at the same time restless. What on earth do I want? The conclusion is clear. I am in bitter conflict with myself — for everything that is a positive thought, the next one is a negative. The two gradually merging into one of grey. Why must I be so afflicted? What is the answer?

Went to Scarborough with Margaret and it did me good, I felt lighter, the mood is passing. Thank God.

Next 3 days the evil of the bottle again. What silliness on reflection, but the compulsion in my case has got to be satisfied.

Sporadic lifts, but still low overall — bad tempered, intolerant to most things. I can't seem to get on with painting at all. It really is a day at a time. I go to bed with the idea that tomorrow I will do this, that and so on, quite enthusiastic - then comes the dawn and the same greyness and futility descends making it — just another day.

And when he was improving:

When immersed in painting I feel very fulfilled. I will discipline myself to work towards a more abundant life with the attendant joys, rather than the miasma of melancholia and the destroyer alcohol.

I am convinced the herbs from Margaret are greatly helping.

For the first time in years I really feel contented. I feel I have now submitted my life to God and he will sustain me in the future. Painted irises in thin wash acrylic, on canvas. Quite pleasing.

It took about eighteen months of AA meetings with lots of setbacks before Ken could call himself a recovering alcoholic. But finally he was free and I was delighted that in April, 1989, a sober and lovely gentleman Ken accompanied me to Torquay where I received my certificate as a fully-qualified member of medical herbalists. I started advertising my services.

In a town ten miles from us, there had been a herbalist for many years. He was popular and there was a constant queue in his waiting room on consultation days. He died, I think it was a heart attack, very suddenly. As a result, his patients saw my advert and were phoning for appointments. That should have been a great start for me, but his methods turned out to be not the same as mine. Patients would describe tastes of medicine and what colour tablets he had given them. They also said he had looked into their eyes and told them that maybe they had liver problems, kidney problems, or needed nerve medicine, and would prescribe according to their eye marks. They were missing him badly and hoped I could give the same treatment as he did because he was so good.

I contacted his daughter, offered my sympathies and asked whether I could perhaps buy his stocks or see his records. I explained my dilemma and arranged to visit her. Neither his daughter nor I could make much sense of his records. He used a code probably known only to himself. The herbs and tablets were from various suppliers such as the long-established Potters Herbals at Wigan. He used mainly mixtures, rather than the single-herb tinctures that I had been taught to mix myself into individual prescriptions. We settled on a price and I bought his stock. I was thankful for having studied Iridology, because it gave his patients confidence when I examined their eyes.

Over the next few months, I learned about all the mixtures and tablets I had acquired and arranged them in my dispensary with the single tinctures. I managed to develop a clinic of herbal medicine and offer acupuncture as well. Alternative medicine was becoming popular. There were two main types of patient. There was a stalwart minority who believed that the body could heal itself and only wanted help from natural medicine such as herbs or life-style changes; and there was the majority who were not getting better, despite the doctor's treatments.

The first consultation would take at least an hour, follow-up appointments half-an-hour. During my studies, I had bought a very basic computer so I could type out my answers for the herbalism course. The printer used a continual fan of paper that was punched longitudinally along both edges that engaged with sprocket wheels, and it was perforated transversely so you could tear off the sheets. I designed and printed my own charts that included all systems of the body, which I used as an aide-memoir during consultations. They also provided a record of treatments.

Depending on the patient's reluctance or pleasure, I would glean information about physical, mental and social/family health, in order to provide the most helpful regime for diet, relaxation and exercise, as well as the herbal prescription. Some preferred to keep the conversation close to their current symptoms, leaving the rest of their life totally private. That worked all right in many cases; symptoms could be relieved and my intuition would help as I wrote out a prescription and dispensed the medicine. Others would be relieved to talk about more aspects of their life so that I could include lots more information as I planned which herbs to use. They would be interested to know why certain herbs were chosen and might even watch as I dispensed them. Most people felt better for taking the herbs and better for talking about themselves.

My intention had been to grow herbs myself and make my own tinctures. Fate decreed differently with the acquisition of the mixtures and patients from the deceased herbalist, so I trusted my suppliers to make the tinctures and gave more thought to the cause and effect of disease. There tended to be confusion between herbalism and homeopathy; I often had to explain the difference. Briefly I would say that herbalism used the whole herb, which could be one part or a mixture of root, bark, leaf, flowers or berries; whereas homeopathy used energy from the herb or maybe mineral or other matter which was diluted in water and alcohol, then shaken and re-diluted repeatedly until there was none of the original properties of the plant or matter left in the formula, except it's energy.

I was very interested in, and read all I could about, Dr Edward Bach, a pathologist and homeopath who identified the flower remedies named after him. He believed that the state of mind was a very important factor in treating disease. One child with measles might want to hide under the bedclothes; another might want to cling to his mother. By treating the state of mind, healing their measles would be easier. There were thirty-eight remedies, each representing negative state of minds. I found these to be most useful as a way of helping patients to identify their mental processes. Whilst I dispensed the herbs, I would often give a leaflet with all the Bach flowers and their negative emotions listed and ask them to tick off any that they related to. An alarming number would think they needed to tick nearly all of them, so we could then discuss the issues and narrow them down to five or six. I would dispense their Bach flower remedies in a dropper bottle and suggest they took them directly on the tongue three times daily.

Ken and I were finally establishing our separate work and enjoying life. Ken fixed himself a studio, where he could paint to his heart's content. He wrote in his diary:

I thank God for his mercy and favours toward me, at last I feel I am on the right road — I am trying to work hard. More and more, I realise that painting is a great joy to me. I look in the AA book and find Hebrews 8:5. Be content with such things as ye have. Does this apply to my picture? I think not, but much more to my now fully accepted way of life.

Ken painted a wonderful copy of *Matisse's Anemones in Earthenware Vase*, which looked well in the dining-room. He copied or styled himself on, Picasso, Caravaggio, Frank Bramley, Van Gogh, Alma Tadema, Peplo and Scottish colorists', Alfred Munnings, and many more. He was a self-taught artist and would challenge himself with new media but had problems working with acrylic paint. He was delighted when David came on one of his visits and demonstrated glazing techniques in acrylic, painting several pictures as examples which he

Mum among her portraits at Vernon Road.

later shared out between Mum, Paul, Ken and me. He brought Mum from Bradford and painted her on the same visit

We had a lot of visitors and soon realised that having a large house at the seaside was an attraction to friends and relatives. We welcomed them, but at times we felt in need of more time and space for ourselves. We made a decision to have a day-off each week, to go together maybe to York or Hull, where we would both do our own thing and then meet for lunch. Bookshops and art galleries were high on our list of things to do.

We certainly did a lot of cooking and bed-making, but it was all pleasant enough and Ken loved the audience for his paintings. He exhibited in a few local art galleries and was proud to have one in the Mall Gallery in London, a multi-perspective painting of Flamborough, which gave him extra pleasure when Paul chose to buy it and hang it on the wall of his Flamborough home.

I was getting up to thirty patients a week, so was kept busy, but not enough to afford extra help. Ken became a bottle washer and telephone answerer as well as artist-in-residence.

Ken's multi-perspective painting of Flamborough Lighthouse 1989.

In July, 1989, my brother John, his wife Helen and her daughter Angela, decided to leave Australia and come to live in York. It was lovely to have them so close. Philip and his wife Mary had already become regular visitors. They made Australia feel quite close. In fact Philip invited a whole group of us to go Down Under for the wedding of his youngest daughter Melanie.

In March, 1990, Ken and I flew to Sydney. David, Paul and Jean were already there. Philip had a beautiful house and grounds, with tennis court, swimming pool, rotunda and well-kept gardens — evidence of how well he had done for himself and his family since emigrating as a 'ten-pounder' all those years ago. The wedding was lovely and was followed by lunch in a marquee covering the tennis court.

After the wedding, Philip arranged that we all tour in two Land Rovers, and had a wonderful holiday that included a visit to Philip's new farm Linden Hills at Harden — a rather grand place with a lake, detached indoor swimming pool and lots of surrounding farmland.

Philip also took us to his factory on the outskirts of Sydney — quite a large and well-organised series of workshops consisting of assembly,

Thomas the tanker: a sticker from Philip.

welding and laser cutting, the main metal in the workshops being aluminium. Back in the offices, all very busy, were typists, draughtsmen and designers. The boardroom was full of interesting aluminium models.

It was a great tour of the factory from raw materials to the end-product of road tanker containers. Philip was just the type of immigrant Australia wanted. He was well-off financially and most generous with his invitations and hospitality. He had three lovely daughters, all now married. We discussed Mum's ninetieth birthday in December. Philip and Mary planned to take the whole family to the celebrations, so it would be quite a big do.

17 The House by the Sea

Fresh sea air at Bridlington

Back home there were problems to be faced. Paul and Jean were finding that Mum was getting very frail, needing more care than they could manage. Jean was becoming anxious and worried about Mum, which was not doing her health any good. Paul said a way of relief would be for John and Helen to take Mum alternate weekends with Ken and me. Well it might help them, but neither Ken nor I thought it was a great solution for us: Ken was just over the alcoholism and I was trying to build up a clinic practice. John and Helen were building their own life, even though Helen was also a trained nurse.

We managed a few weekends, but it was not a long-term answer. Mum needed more help with everyday tasks, cooking, washing, shopping and walking in the fresh air, which she looked forward to every day come rain or shine. Her care at home was fragmented, reliant on neighbours and friends as well as Jean and Paul and their four children. Paul organised a few changes in the kitchen to make it easier and safer to use. She already had an easy access shower and lightweight kettle jug. I dispensed herbs and Bach flower remedies to help ease her aches and pains. I also made herbs to try and help Jean, and any other family member with problems.

Mum had plenty of interesting happenings that she could enjoy. Her grandchildren were having babies and christenings. Philip and Mary came again to visit after they had entertained us all in Australia. The newly-weds, Melanie and John, visited as well. David came back or made phone calls regularly and Mum would phone her friends and get car lifts to visit them. And of course Paul and Jean continued to support and help her, as they had been doing for years.

Her ninetieth birthday was approaching on December 10 and a couple of parties were planned. Then David dropped a bombshell. He phoned his mother in late November to say that he had been in hospital for some tests to do with indigestion. He said it might have been a mild heart-attack. The doctor advised him not to travel yet. He phoned Ken and me, asking if we would go over to Los Angeles for Christmas with Mum, so he would not have to travel into winter. So there was an enormous and good family birthday party with everyone there except David.

Paul made the travel arrangements and saw us off at the airport on 19, December to join David in California. We had a lovely Christmas between David's main residence at Montcalm in the Hollywood Hills, and down in the beach-house at Malibu. He was creating the sets for the Turandot opera that was opening in Chicago early in 1992. Philip, Mary and family arrived on New Year's Eve, on their way home to Australia. We all enjoyed time together, watching Mum's birthday video as well as Turandot. The Australians continued on their world tour, travelling home a few days later. David had made a good recovery and his energy was extraordinary: after half-an-hour's rest he would

Mum's ninetieth birthday. Left to right: Helen and John, Jean and Paul, Mum, Mary and Philip, me and Ken.

transform from weary and tired, to happy and full of energy. As we left for the airport to return home, he was off to New York for the Magic Flute opera opening.

John and Helen met us at Leeds-Bradford airport and took us to Mum's house in Eccleshill. Next day we called to see them in York on our way up to Bridlington. We were most surprised and disappointed to hear that John was thinking of selling-up and going back to Australia. He said there were work problems for both him and Helen. By May they were gone.

Meanwhile Mum needed more help. Ken and I did what we could, but my practice was getting busier. Our weekly day-off increasingly became a day in Bradford to take Mum out. One such trip was to the National Museum of Photography, Film and Television, as it was then called, where David had an exhibition of his digital joiner-photographs. We also took her to Salts Mill quite frequently, where we were welcomed by Jonathan Silver. Mum had first met Jonathan, his brother Robin and their wives Maggie and Pat in 1980 when they invited her to Manchester for an exhibition of David's work from the 1960's. In 1987 Jonathan bought Salts Mill, the huge redundant textile mill in Saltaire, near Bradford, where he set up a permanent exhibition of David's pictures. The first time Ken and I visited Salts Mill with Mum, Jonathan asked her if she had any pictures he could have on loan to start filling his wall space. She thought there were a few he could borrow. Ken and I drove Mum leisurely home and were amazed to see that Jonathan was already waiting at her house for the pictures. We soon got to know what a whizz of a man he was. A most caring person if you got to know him, he was a hard grafter with great vision, determination and success. Salts Mill 1853 Gallery developed and became a regular place to visit and enjoy.

Paul had a sixtieth birthday party in May. Philip and Mary came again from Australia to join the party. Philip had been working on a new straight-sided oil tanker called THOMAS, (Tanker Having Optimum Mass And Stability). He showed us a film of this amazing vehicle. I felt thrilled a few weeks later when I saw one of his tankers at Safeway's supermarket in Bridlington delivering petrol. We collected and drove Mum to Paul's party; she was looking really frail and needing more help than ever. She was also becoming unsteady on her feet.

As we drove home, Ken and I began to formulate an idea of Mum coming to live with us in Bridlington if we could get a suitable house. Vernon Road suited us fine but there were a lot of steps. Even on weekend visits Mum was not happy with those steps. I had always said that if she died first I would care for Dad - my brothers thought that he was the awkward one - but I did not think I could cope with Mum. I believed I was not really the daughter she hoped for: she had powerful emotional energy but she thought I was hard and uncaring.

Ken got on fine with Mum and with all the family. Without his support I could not have entertained the idea of her living with me. We discussed how the arrangement might work and whether we could manage. Although Mum was looking frail, Ken and I reckoned that with regular home-cooked meals - Mum was a lifelong vegetarian - and a safe environment, Mum had enough inner-strength that could enable her to live a good few years yet. We decided to take the plunge. I phoned Mum to hear what she thought and also sent a fax of a possible property on Sewerby cliff.

Quickly, the idea took hold with Mum, Paul, Philip, David and John. The first property was unsuitable. We then viewed a large house in

Kingston Road that was being used as a hotel which, subject to planning consent, could revert for residential living. There was a self-contained flat suitable for Mum and plenty of bedrooms for family and friends to stay. There was space to make a new clinic for me and a studio in the loft for Ken and David. The sea and beach were just across the road.

I would have to continue working at Vernon Road until a new clinic was ready but it was only a short drive away. I faxed the details to my brothers. They would sort out the finance until I could add my chip when I sold the Vernon Road house and moved to my new clinic. Mum would probably need a nurse each day to help her get up because I started my work early. Mum faxed that she was thrilled at the prospect of moving to Bridlington, in a suitable house.

She wrote in her diary:

David phoned about 7, had been speaking to Margaret. He is very keen, and thinks I would like the new premises at Bridlington, and can make my home there. I am so thankful and overwhelmed that our dear children so care for me now that I am old, God bless them all. HE has blessed me. I wait HIS will.

Ken and I told the family that we hoped Mum would still remain as independent as possible, also that we hoped to continue to have a day-off every week to visit neighbouring towns — depending on Mum's needs. We would be attending an annual herbal conference lasting a few days.

On December 7, 1991, the sale of 31 Kingston Road was completed and belonged to me. Ken and I moved in and brought Mum a few days later. We settled her into the warm cosy flat and arranged that a lovely nurse, Yvonne, would visit daily to wash and dress her. Yvonne did much more than that and became Mum's reliable and companionable friend. Mum's ground floor-flat was across a marble-floored vestibule opposite the front door. The main house had a spacious hall, dining room, kitchen and lounge. There was a balconied landing leading to six bedrooms, three of them en-suite, and a main bathroom. There was room for my clinic. The house by the sea would become a family home where friends and relatives could stay as long as they wished when they visited Mum.

David loved the house and saw great potential in the spacious rooms and en-suite bedrooms. David was like Ken and me: he enjoyed his own private space between socialising. There was a massive loft area that he reckoned would make a wonderful studio. So we had builders in to convert that space and construct a wide staircase to accommodate the movement of large canvases. The studio would be fantastic with good North light and a view to Bridlington harbour. Philip, the family draughtsman, came up with a marvellous idea of converting an integral garage at one side of the house into a clinic with a private side-entrance. There was already a double-garage at the other side and plenty of parking spaces, so his idea worked really well. The hotel would become a lovely home including Mum's flat, my clinic and a big studio for Ken and David.

David and his friend Jonathan Brown stayed for that first Christmas. Paul, Jean and their family joined us for a large Boxing Day buffet. During Christmas, Mum had two falls in the hall. She was bruised and upset, but nothing was broken. Trouble was that she was forgetting her age, rushing from her flat to the main house wondering what David was doing. Ken, me and the nurse were taking her out for daily walks along the promenade, but she got very tired and did not seem aware of her more limited mobility. She was hoping to go shopping, do some sewing, walk on her own, help us with cooking and of course was missing the neighbours and grandchildren from Bradford who used to pop in so frequently. She was still adapting to her new home, surroundings and daily routines. Yvonne would pick her up manually, all seven-stone of her, and put her in a lovely foamy bath - an absolute luxury that Mum appreciated very much. She chose a more comfortable wheelchair than the Red Cross one we had loaned. I fixed her up with a new telephone with twenty speed dials. Social services organised a Lifeline neck button to use for emergencies.

David had designed the sets for Puccini's Turandot at the Chicago Lyric Opera. He invited Ken and I to the opening in mid-January 1992. We stayed three nights. The opera was stupendous and the sets brilliant. Mum was not happy about us going away and was most agitated when we suggested she stayed in a nursing-home for the few days. Ken's sister Annie and her friend Barbara came to the rescue: they agreed to stay in the house to cook and be company for Mum. They, or my cousin and his wife, said they would stay to relieve us when we were on the herbal conference breaks. Several months of building surveys, architecture plans and form-filling passed before planning permission was granted to build my surgery and convert the loft space

for a studio. I continued working at Vernon Road.

To begin with Ken and I would have our evening meal in the flat
with Mum. The main house was too cold for her and her flat was really
too hot for us. There was a table in her kitchen adjoining her sitting-
room, but Mum preferred to eat on a small table near her sitting-room
fire. She did not like us eating in her kitchen because she said we were
not being sociable. After a few months of Ken and I eating from our
knees, we said the posture was not good for our digestion. We changed
the routine by delivering her meal, then eating ours in the main dining
room.

Mum was really keen to make a birthday cake for David, and said,
'It seems such a waste in this cosy flat with all conveniences, that I am
unable to use them to bake cake.' So
Ken and I made a Dundee cake in
her oven, in her kitchen, and she
thought it turned out beautifully.

Philip and John came with their
families from Australia. David would
bring many friends. These visits
made Mum very happy. Paul and
Jean, who had a holiday home at
Flamborough Head just a few miles
away, were regular callers at Kingston
Road. Her grandchildren would
bring their babies for the day. Two
ladies from nearby Sewerby
Methodist Chapel called frequently
and Mum had friends stay over from
Bradford. Ken and I took her on
necessary visits to buy new furniture
and to visit the consultant about her
arthritic hip. We took her to Hull,

David with his birthday cake, made in Mum's
kitchen and iced by Ken.

Bradford, Scarborough and the lovely cafe at Oliver's Mount. Yvonne
was very kind and took her out in her car.

Finally Mum sold her house in Bradford to continue her new life-
style.

The building work of clinic and studio lasted nearly two years. There
would be a permanent rubbish skip outside and workmen banging,

sawing, cutting off the electric or water and generally filling the house with dust and activity. Ken and I were both early risers. Cooking, baking, washing and other household chores would be done between 4am and 6am. We walked the dogs and had breakfast by 7am. I was busy working in the clinic at Vernon Road till late afternoon. Ken was often frustrated that he couldn't get on with his painting because of all the workmen. Mum would phone Ken and he would sit and talk with her whilst she told him about her aches and pains. Her irritable bowel was involving Ken and I, as well as the nurse. She would have accidents and need help to clean up and change clothing. When David was on the horizon for visiting or phoning she got agitated with excitement, I would give her Bach flower Rescue Remedy. It sometimes helped. For the first couple of years I helped Mum to get ready for bed, but the workmen and the dust and the constant visitors, domestic work and running the clinic began to have a toll on me. I would get very tired and have a troublesome cough. Mum wanted to go to bed later than me and she wasn't too happy at wearing her nightclothes by 7pm. She wanted me to wait till at least 8.30 pm. The solution was for Yvonne to return in the evening and put Mum to bed.

A worry to Mum was when Yvonne went on holiday. There would be a relief nurse, but not the same as Yvonne. Mum continued to read her Bible every day, so Ken quoted:

Matthew 6:31-3,4 Therefore do not be anxious about tomorrow, for tomorrow will be anxious for itself. Sufficient for the day is its own trouble.

She wasn't too keen for us to give Bible quotes. I suppose she thought we were hypocrites.

In 1993 I started mixing up names and numbers when I listened to the telephone. I tried different phones and hearing gadgets but voices were no longer clear enough to trust my hearing. Ken took over all the phone calls, and I just used the fax machine. In February 1993 John was seriously ill in hospital. He had septicaemia and remained in hospital several weeks, but eventually made a good recovery. He was discharged early in April. We faxed his wife Helen in Australia to keep up with reports. David flew over to visit him. Although the time was worrying the fax was a wonderful means of communicating: David called it a telephone for the deaf. As part of John's convalescence, at David's suggestion, he visited us for two months to archive the letters and memorabilia of Dad that had been stored in Eccleshill and taken

to Vernon Road. There was a lot to be sorted.

John did a good job of cataloguing and arranging the archived items. We would laugh at some of Dad's letters and posters, sometimes wondering whether his collected memorabilia was just a load of old rubbish, which a lot of it was. There were: photographs titled with sticky labels, some were labelled spoiled or under-exposed; old records of Sunday School classes from the 1930s along with topics of sermons; photos of men on the moon taken from TV; enormous home-made scrap books made of hardboard filled with brown paper sheets held together with industrial-sized lever-arch binder clips. The scrap books were full of newspaper cuttings including some of David, others of Paul during his Lord Mayor year. Dad had used an old typewriter to bash out his many letters: it had a double-colour ribbon and he would keep copies of everything he sent. John had organised the memorabilia into categories piled on the large sitting-room floor at Vernon Road. Headings included religion, morals, politics, crime, sex, health, smoking, alcohol, child-abuse, prison systems and war photographs. Dad was nothing if not eclectic.

I told John that I had offered to help Mum write her own story from all the diaries she had compiled during many years of her life. I lent her an electronic typewriter to do it herself. She managed to write a couple of letters to friends, easier than hand-writing with her painful hands, but decided the typewriter was too fast for her. She showed me a diary from the 1950s and said I could type it on my computer. My intention had been to suggest something she might enjoy doing. I was willing to help but was far too busy to do it myself. This was the first time I had seen what she had written in her diary. There was a whole suitcase full of them and at the back of each were pages to keep accounts of income and expenditure. All were neatly filled-in. I put the 1950's one back in her suitcase.

John and I reminisced about when we were younger and started writing diaries. One Christmas we had both been given five-year diaries each of which had its own lock and key. I told him that Mum had unlocked mine and commented on something I had written. Once I knew the diary wasn't private I never wrote in one again. The same happened to John. We had always known that Mum wrote her daily diary. She would keep it in the sideboard drawer but it was sacrosanct. I had no idea what she was writing; and I don't think any of my brothers or Dad would ever have dared to look either. We talked of the letters that Mum had always asked us to write. John was surprised when I told him they had been saved in another suitcase. I hadn't opened it but Mum told me they were all there.

We jokingly agreed there would be enough material to write a book from all these memory-joggers and looked forward someday to browsing through them. The result of my browsing is this book that I started writing in the year 2016. I did find it rather strange that Mum wrote detailed diaries in 1925 and 1926, when she first met Dad as a Sunday-School teacher. Very abruptly in February, 1927, there are no more diary entries: nothing whatsoever about her courtship with Dad. The diaries started again in the late 1940s and continued into the early 1990s. A pity I only discovered that after she had died.

18 An Aged Parent

In October, 1993, Mum had a hip-replacement in Scarborough Hospital. When she came round from the anaesthetic she thought one of her babies had just been delivered. Two weeks later she returned home, walking, eating and healing well. I finally moved into my new clinic at the end of 1993. There was a side-entrance separate from the main house, a small waiting room with toilet, an adequate consulting-room with my desk placed so I had the daylight behind me to aid lip-reading. The wooden doors were stained green and had flowered knobs. The carpet was green and the walls cream. I took the wooden couch and furniture from Vernon Road. A staircase led to the dispensary and computer room. It was perfect, a marvellous place to work.

Despite having a wonderful nurse in Yvonne, Mum often felt we should be doing more for her. She wanted to join us on our days out and could not understand that our need for freedom and solitude was as important to us as her daily Bible reading was to her. She didn't see such things the same as we did. Possibly I reminded Mum of Dad. She wanted more from me than there actually was of me. I did say to her that even though I might not be the daughter she hoped for, I would never turn her out of our home: she could stay forever unless she chose otherwise. David made regular visits and would always paint or draw

Old remedies renewed.

'I wonder where David is?'.

Mum and maybe Ken and me. When he left, Mum would say that she never had David to herself. She wanted more of him too. David does not converse when he is doing portraits, so Mum would sit attentively but not be able to talk with him.

In February, 1994, Mum had been very anxious and disgruntled with her life. She became physically ill and stayed in bed with abdominal pain, no appetite and vomiting small amounts of bile. The doctor visited and within a few days admitted her to Scarborough Hospital. Investigations were carried out with no definite diagnosis, so she had exploratory abdominal surgery. A small perforation was repaired, but no other problems were found. She made a good recovery but had a few nightmares of ghosts and her own funeral. Jim, an old friend and Methodist Minister, went to talk with her about the nightmares; but she did not want to listen to him, said 'he has his God, I have mine.' She had lots of visitors whilst in hospital. David drew her and sent flowers. After two weeks she returned home with a good appetite and well-recovered.

A few weeks later Philip visited and told us that he had been diagnosed with prostate cancer. He was taking homeopathic remedies but might need surgery when he returned to Australia. Rather selfishly Mum hinted to Philip: 'It's a long time since I was in an aeroplane. I've never been in Paul's new car. Margaret and Ken don't take me out with them very often. I'm all-alone in this big house'. She emphasised her complaints with tearfulness. Philip spent time with her and compared her facilities with the more frugal life of his mother-in-law. Neither of them seemed too happy at growing old.

Philip had his surgery. There were a few post-operative complications that he reported by fax with engineering terms as though his body was one of his tankers: 'Report on repairs to: — Hockney Body'. He always had a great sense of humour and was full of good ideas. He made an excellent recovery. When he retired from his business he went on to buy and revive an ailing supermarket in Harden and also became Mayor of the town. In June 1995 we got a fax from Philip to say he has been awarded the Order of Australia. It was a great honour. A few days later David was awarded Doctor of Letters from Oxford University.

Ken and I continued with our weekly days out and for the first five minutes of driving we might be cursing something that Mum said or did, then one of us would count — one, two, three — and we both would scream in the privacy of the car and change the subject. Some days the subject might be why the sky is blue or the grass green. Well, grass was not always green and even when it was there were so many hues and tones the subject could fill a conversation. Other topics included eternity, space and time. Having mastered the wisdom of 'one day at a time' and 'there is only today', we would observe today in the great scheme of things. We would relate this to the daily chores, workmen raising dust all over the house, awkward relationships and, for a time, these worries would dissolve and become unimportant. When we reached York or Hull we could enjoy our time in bookshops, art galleries or just doing nothing in particular.

Getting any closer to my Mother was difficult; she was such a strong emotional force in my life. I wrote a rather long dissertation, which I gave to each of my brothers, titled: My Mother is Not Your Mother. The essence of it was:

When I was 10 years old I was talking with a school friend I used to visit. She told me that if her mother should die, well she would die too, because life would be unbearable without her mother. That was the first day I considered that mothers did die, and far from being unbearable, I realised there could be a surge of freedom, and to this day I am aware I cannot be my true self as long as my mother exists. It doesn't matter all that much. Not many, if any of us, are our true selves all the time and maybe I will never feel totally free anyway.

I realised what a dreadfully strong power my mother had on me. She was probably quite unaware of this.

Human energy is like trillions of magnets, each one attracting or repelling within the individual to maintain equilibrium of life itself. There could be a long discourse on how the energy arises from food, air, metabolism, emotions, but suffice to say it keeps us moving and living.

Relationships with other humans or for that matter any other animal or thing, involve the mutual attraction or repellence of energy. As we have so much energy, we can usually put on a good act of tolerance, rather than total repellence or fear. However, as we all know, relationships can reach a state of intolerance, where all 'magnets' seem to repel. There are usually a few attractive magnets too, so there is a lot of conflict involved.

I do not blame my mother because I feel more repelling magnets than attracting ones. I find her energy far too strong to cope with so am constantly 'backing away' from her.

During the last ten years I have done a lot of studying, and had some vital experience, especially relating to Ken. Yes! Thank God for Ken. He had problems of his own, which I learnt to realise were his problems. My problem was feeling hurt and angry because of his problem. I learned how to overcome that — learnt a lot of philosophy — a firm favourite is 'Let Go Let God'. Very profound when used literally, by leaving go of God and not by God bothering. Incidentally I class God as energy, or a Power greater than me, not as a father in heaven!

Ken talked on my wavelength. At last I had found a soul mate. He understood my conflict, did not condemn or advise, but just understood. What more could one want?

I bear no hatred or grudge to any living creature, least of all my mother. This is the reason, that when Ken and I saw that OUR (Paul, Philip, David and John and my) MOTHER was becoming unable to look after herself we suggested getting a house large enough for us all to have our own space where she could be safely cared for, and where the family and friends could visit her, and sleep under the same roof. I knew the magnetism was still a problem, in so much as there would be no physical closeness, and certainly no involvement with my working situation, but there is plenty of common sense, knowledge, and the supporting help and humour of Ken. True we had to rely on finance from elsewhere, I can offer only what is within my means, and that is what I do now. If this situation is not acceptable to any of you, then please suggest an alternative.

They read it and hopefully understood more about my difficult relationship with Mum.

In September, 1995, Jonathan Silver — the owner of Salts Mill — phoned with grave news. He had been diagnosed with a tumour of the pancreas. We were all devastated. David went off to visit him. He did get the all-clear for a while, and would drive over to see David and have his portrait painted. He was most kind and generous, often bringing gifts of flowers or books.

On my sixtieth birthday I videoed David and Ken painting lamb chops in the studio. More importantly I started getting the old-age pension. I was still working so decided to put the pension money to memorable use by purchasing a computerised sewing machine and an over-locker machine. I learnt many sewing techniques and made cushions, curtains, bedspreads as well as clothing and doing repair jobs. I even got a highly-commended rosette for my wearable-art jacket entry in a national competition and enjoyed seeing it on display at Olympia in London. I had a marvellous shopping spree for fabrics when Liberty's had a closing-down sale in York.

In May, 1996, Paul and Jean sold their house in Bradford to make their permanent home in Flamborough. They had had property in Flamborough for many years, but it was just used for holidays. Mum got quite excited and had high hopes of a better social life with them. Unfortunately, shortly after they moved, Jean's mother had a stroke and was admitted to a nursing home. Jean and Paul visited her back in Bradford two or three times a week for the next six years.

Mum was still being difficult even with Yvonne who was the most caring nurse she would ever get. Yvonne was going on a week's holiday and we decided to let Mum go in a local nursing home for the week. Yvonne took her and surprisingly there was not too much fuss. When she came back home however she did object and said did not want to go there again.

At the end of April, Ken and I went to London to see David's *Flower and Portrait* exhibition at Anely Juda gallery. Mum was not at all happy that she had to go into Rosegarth nursing home again, two streets away from Kingston Road, a clean respectable home with good caring staff. David's show was on May 1, the day of the General Election when Tony Blair's New Labour Party was voted in. Later, as we walked to dinner, Ken and I were stopped by a woman in Bond Street. She asked where I had got my 'divine jacket.' When I told her it was homemade she was most intrigued. That boosted my confidence in my sewing abilities.

On May 25, 1997, David showed us a letter from the Prime Minister, Downing Street, to say he had been nominated for Companion of Honour (CH). He said he would accept and the ceremony was on July 30. Paul took Mum and Yvonne to stay two nights at the Ritz hotel for that memorable visit to Buckingham palace. Fifteen years later in 2012, David also received the Order of Merit (OM) from the Queen. Unlike other honours, the OM is the personal gift of the Monarch.

Meanwhile Jonathan was very ill again. He had amazing energy and would still drive over for David to paint him and bring flowers and gifts. As he continued to decline in health David spent the next three months mainly living with us in Bridlington. He painted pictures of Yorkshire to take when he visited Jonathan at his home in Wetherby to cheer him up. Driving across the Wolds via Sledmere and Garrowby

Hill he was aware of the landscape and the big skies above East
Yorkshire. Many years ago when we went farming during school holidays David's favourite place had been at Huggate near Wetwang, where
he had helped with harvesting as a youngster. In those days he would
cycle from Bradford and enjoy the smoke-free fresh air as he cycled
through York and into East Yorkshire. What with those memories and
Jonathan's suggestion, he told Ken and me that he would come back
soon and 'paint Yorkshire'. David had many visitors staying and supporting him. We were very busy with the cooking and housekeeping
as we welcomed his guests. Mum was desperately trying to get more
attention from David, saying he spent too much time with Jonathan.
Maybe she was not fully aware of the tragic circumstances. David
continued to paint her; sometimes you could see the anger and resentment in her face. Jonathan and Maggie Silver had been so kind to Mum
that it was embarrassing to see this sort of selfish behaviour. We had
to ignore her to preserve our own peace of mind.

Yvonne and her family went on holiday for two weeks in August.
Life was far too busy to cope with Mum and her complaints, so we
arranged that she go into Rosegarth for the duration. This did not
please her at all. She would be leaving David with us and she told him
that she did not want to go there. It is one the very few times that I saw
David lose patience with her. He had just got news that Jonathan had
only five weeks to live. We all visited Mum during her time at Rosegarth. She was well-cared for but not happy. On August 31 David went
to visit. She was still grumbling about being away from us all. He told
her the shocking news that Princess Diana had been killed in Paris
with Dodi Fayed. Yes awful isn't it she said. Is there any more tea in
that pot? As we watched the funeral of Diana, Ken and I recalled that
soon after we met we watched the wedding of her and Prince Charles,
sixteen years before.

David had a forthcoming photography retrospective exhibition in
December 1997 in Cologne. This involved many visits to us by
exhibition staff to sort out portfolios for the show. It was a busy time
and Ken and I were never quite sure how many visitors would be arriving or leaving. The cooker was playing up and we decided to get a new
one as soon as all was quiet again. David said, 'why not have a new
kitchen?' Well we couldn't afford a new kitchen. But David enjoyed the
house very much and said a new kitchen would be an enhancement.

We had been managing to cook in quite a small space so plans were set in action to make a nice spacious kitchen.

On September 25, 1997, Jonathan Silver died. It was a sad day for all of us. David went to the funeral next day — a private affair. He told us that en-route back to Bridlington he had given himself a quiet moment of reflection in York Minster. He planned to return to Los Angeles in a few days. The day before David left, Ken had a varicose vein operation and hoped he would get relief from the pain he had been suffering for the past year.

We were still busy after David left. All the paintings he had done were photographed, catalogued and taken away. This involved three people over a week or so. Ken tidied up the studio and cleaned eighty-four paintbrushes. I was very busy in the clinic. There was lots of tidying up around the house to be done and we had plans set out for the new kitchen. Yvonne was not very well and Mum was complaining again that I should be giving her more help. Ken and I desperately needed a break and planned to go to London for a few days as soon as Ken had the clips out from his operation. We decided to admit Mum to Rosegarth whilst we were away. Talk about kicking and screaming. The hate and resentment that flowed out of Mum was unbelievable.

The London break helped us to relax and we chose some appliances for the new kitchen. Back home Mum was far from relaxed. She could see no reason why she had been in the nursing home and blamed Ken and me for everything wrong in her life. Mum continued to complain to all and sundry including Philip. She phoned him in Australia saying how unhappy she was. He sent a fax to both Mum and us suggesting that she should dwell permanently in Rosegarth, leaving me and Ken to live peacefully on our own. There were many phone calls and discussions about this between Paul, Philip and David. Finally the decision was made and Rosegarth agreed to admit her. We took her on November 25, 1997. None of us were really happy and Mum was most tearful. Next day we visited her but wished we hadn't bothered. She was absolutely dreadful. 'Take me home. Take me out in the chair. Do this. Do that. Get my coat.' The lady in the room with her did not look happy. We were not sure whether the staff could manage her. Mum seemed so wild.

I had not been feeling at all well, having dizzy spells and headaches. My blood-pressure was yo-yoing up and down, but I knew the reason was my busy life so did not seek any medical advice. Paul suggested we go with him to Cologne for David's photograph exhibition. Jean would not be going. He arranged the tickets and accommodation. We flew from Humberside airport and had a thoroughly happy few days. David's exhibition was a great success; especially interesting was his photographic joiner of The Grand Canyon. We met many people and had a splendid dinner. John and Helen were there from Australia and we joined them as we toured the shops, the Cathedral and the Christmas market.

John and Helen joined us for Christmas, as did David and two of his friends. Mum came for the lunch and enjoyed the presents and decorations. On Boxing Day we had the usual buffet. We had one the whole time we were at Kingston Road. Neighbours, friends, Paul's family and some of John's friends, about forty people in all came to the house. Paul arranged the games and there were carols sung in the

Me and Ken hosting again.

grandly-decorated hall. Paul's youngest son Nick played the organ. Mum looked rather miserable despite all the attention she was getting.

After Christmas the builders moved in to make the new kitchen. Ken and I moved into the kitchen in the flat. Mum was still complaining that she should not be in a nursing home when she had five children. We decided to visit less often. We were hoping that there would soon be a single room available for her. She was slightly happier when she was moved to one and gradually began to accept her life with twenty-four hour care and attention. She was helped to walk and join other residents for meals in the dining room and go on occasional bus tours.

Our new kitchen was finished by June. We had a built-in steam oven which I used daily to steam the organic vegetables that I bought locally. There was a jumbo oven for when David and his friends wanted a dozen grouse cooking or a whole roast dinner. Working in such a kitchen was a pleasure.

David was very stimulated after seeing an Ingres exhibition and was using a *camera lucida* to try out a theory he had. He would send us faxes of his ideas and examples. It was all most interesting.

19 The last Days

The habit of getting up at four in the morning to cook was a hard one to break. Blood pressure was up and down and so long as it went down I was not too worried. Many years before I had completed a course on Transcendental Meditation, but had not heard what the mantra was; in fact I hadn't heard much at all throughout the series of talks. So even though it was expensive I decided to try again. Ken phoned the teacher in Hull to explain my hearing difficulties and we arranged that I would have a few private sessions before joining the group. I duly did the course and set aside twenty minutes morning and evening to meditate. After several weeks I decided it was not helping at all. I would feel as though I were going to have a spontaneous combustion rather than peaceful meditations and had to abandon that idea. I went for longer walks instead, along the beach and around the woods at Danes Dyke.

South beach Bridlington.

There had been many visitors over the last few months of David's visit. I was not able to hear voices when there were more than one or two people talking. Apart from a cacophony of useless noise, I didn't hear much conversation at all round the dining table. I thought that maybe the tension of trying to hear could have been causing my dizziness and unstable blood-pressure. I was also having more difficulty hearing patients, which was very worrying. Our pensions were not sufficient to retire on and run the house. We wondered what to do for the best. David suggested that because he had a bedroom and art materials stored with us he could pay rent. That would help to cover the house maintenance and I could finish working. That was a great relief. I sent a letter to all patients in my register to say I would be retiring in six months, on October 11, 1998. That would give them time to find another herbalist.

I felt a bit sad at having to retire. I had very much enjoyed the herbalism and acupuncture, but the deafness was defeating me again. I was lucky to have worked sixteen years since taking early retirement from nursing. I wondered what next? I told Mum that I would be finishing work. She wasn't interested. 'Where is Paul? Where is David?' she asked.

Ken had not been well since his vein operation. He was found to have two hernias that needed surgery. We had another busy Christmas and the usual Boxing Day buffet. We brought Mum round to join us and she seemed more content, happy to sit in her chair by the fire. David visited her at Rosegarth in February, 1999, and painted three very good portraits of her. She looked peaceful at last. The hardness had gone from her face. In March, Ken had the hernia operation. I decided to get myself a retirement present of a new computer. In early May I ordered a top-of-the-range system that would include the computer, printer, scanner, digital camera and lots of peripheral and software extras. It would be delivered on May 11, 1999.

Ken and I went to tell Mum about the computer. She looked very frail and sleepy but was peaceful and to our delight she smiled in recognition. We knew her end was near. John had been on a lone walkabout in Australia when Dad died in 1979, so felt that he never said goodbye. He had asked us to make sure we warned him so he could say goodbye to Mum before she died. We contacted both David and John to tell that Mum's end was in sight. David booked a flight on Concorde, but on the day the flight was cancelled. He managed to get another one and phoned us when he reached London to say he was on his way to Bridlington. He arrived on the Sunday afternoon. John faxed details of his journey from Australia: he was due to arrive on the Tuesday.

Monday was a day of waiting and watching. David sat with Mum most of the day. He had a short nap and a snack and then returned at midnight. Ken and I had supper with Jean and Paul and then we all sat with Mum whilst David had his nap. Mum was sinking fast, but we told her that John was on his way from Australia and would really love to have a chat with her. We kept updating her about his itinerary and I am absolutely sure that she waited for him. In the evening of Monday there was a thunder and lightning storm and the most beautiful rainbow — as if to say 'look, the gate is open, come'. Ken and I found it very emotive; we thought Mum was going at last to that land where there is no bitterness or pain — into the light of pure love. David and I sat beside her the whole of Monday night, reassuring her that John would not be long and we were all looking forward to seeing him. Finally at 10am on Tuesday we could report that Paul had met John off the train in York and they were on their way for the final forty miles of John's twelve thousand mile journey. Mum waited for him. He arrived at 11am and spent about five hours with her.

David needed to go to London to a meeting at the Royal Academy. Ken and I drove him to York station from where he got the London train. Our minds were all pre-occupied with Mum but we were relieved that John was with her. The drive back from York was like being in a perpetual car wash. There was thunder, lightning and torrential rain all the way. Talk about the heavens opening. We were back in Bridling-ton at 4.15 pm and walked round to Rosegarth, meeting John on our way. He was going for a much-needed rest and told us Paul was now with Mum. We arrived to find Paul with the nurse who was trying to feel Mum's pulse. There was no pulse; she had died at 4.30 pm. We went to get John, then all of us stood a while watching, very sad, but she looked so old and tired, yet peaceful. We broke the news to David and to Philip in Australia. It was so memorable and touching to know that she had waited for John, let him leave her in peace, then go to her next world and whatever it held. We could say that Mum had finally been promoted, hopefully to meet her Saviour.

My computer was delivered the same day, May 11.

20 Going Digital

After the funeral we spent time with David in London. He was still enthused with the camera lucida and doing drawings. We went to the Royal Academy dinner before the Summer Exhibition and he looked very smart wearing the CH ribbon and medal. Life with David in London was fast and fascinating: taxis instead of buses, Ivy restaurant instead of M&S ready-meals. He drove us to Greenwich in his open-top car to see the camera obscura. We visited and met lots of interesting people and went to art galleries. All too soon we had to return to Bridlington.

Scanned hedgerow flowers.

Now was the time to really check out all the computer equipment that I had hastily unpacked but not yet worked out how to use. Getting on the Internet was wonderful. Ken sorted out the studio ready to start painting. We felt so free and relaxed in the house and looked forward to our future life. I did have early problems with the computer. What a job it was getting help. Ken would phone the helpline and explain that I was deaf but would tell them the problem. I then told the helper what the problem was and handed the phone back to Ken for a solution. The situation was a nightmare and could take hours to get the computer up-and-running again. I intensified my search for information websites and tried to learn about all that could go wrong. I needed to manage without having to make phone calls. I joined several online discussion groups where people were discussing the sort of problems I was having. Paul bought the same computer system as me, so I was able to help him set it up. Helping others, I realised, was a great way to learn and remember.

I found good websites to learn about computing, photography and

HTML — the language of website-making. I joined a discussion website called thirdage.com where I talked photography, computer graphics and similar topics. By December I had made Christmas cards on the computer that reversed to a Millennium greeting. I also made several websites that I needed for the online courses I was taking. I was soon spending many hours learning about software and computers in general. I was feeling much better, no more dizziness and my blood pressure settled: the computer life was suiting me. In March I started making a website for Salts Mill and by July it was active online. I had also made websites for two friends using the software that came with the computer. With the thought of possible payment I bought Dream Weaver, a luxury web development tool. I took courses to learn how to use it as well as Flash for movies. This enabled me to be far more adventurous with the websites. I added music to the opera sets on Salts website and made the hundred and forty-four piece fax picture that David had faxed to Jonathan from Los Angeles on the wall into a jigsaw puzzle, using the mouse to drag the pieces into place. Sadly, I was not well enough a few years later to maintain that website.

Salts Mill had a new exhibition of David's opera sets in July and David stayed a few days. He started painting Garrowby Hill: I took close-up photos of sections of his painting with my digital camera and printed them. He was interested in this way of using the camera.

As well as computing I carried on sewing. David invited us to the opening night at Glyndebourne to see the *Rake's Progress* for which he had made the sets. I got busy sewing an outfit for the event. It was a beautiful evening, the sets and opera were marvellous and we had a lovely picnic in the grounds.

David was still busy working on his theories of lenses, mirrors and camera lucida for the book and film *Secret Knowledge*. He had done lots of drawings and paintings to test his idea including painting the attendants of the National Gallery. He invited us on a trip to Bruges for part of his research. We went by car and crossed on the Dover ferry, staying three nights. There was a full day with the BBC filming in a tent in the fish market.

It was a most lively and fun day — Ken sat posing whilst smoking his pipe for part of film. The next day we were met by Professor Charles Falco, an American physicist who shared David's theory of optics in

Ken posing for *Secret knowledge* experiment.

art. Filming was in Ghent cathedral where the Van Eyck Altarpiece is displayed.

Ken was having problems with the hernia wound not healing and he had a repeat operation in December. The wound still didn't heal and in May Ken went for yet another operation. Six months later Ken still had pain in the groin, was not sleeping well and lost weight from his already slender frame. He did not feel as energetic as he used to be. He even wondered whether he had, 'the big C'. He said: 'Life has never been so easy for me except for these looney symptoms. I feel at last I am painting subjects very dear to me. The eyes and aching back remind me that I am nearly 75. Is it too late to enjoy painting? No it bloody well is not. Just get on with it and thank your lucky stars.'

Six months later the hernia was still there so Ken went back to the clinic to find the truth of his problem. He had a scan that showed a haematoma and some mesh structures, but there was nothing sinister and no cancer. He wrote in his diary:

The fears and emotions I have been through I now want to put away and get on with what is left of life. I must confess I was heartily sick of telling people my symptoms, but above all the fear of dying without having done anything. It's quite ridiculous really because I don't think I am going to do anything spectacular anyway, but I have had a most frightening week. I hope I can now put it behind me and start living again.

Two years from Mum dying and me getting the computer, I was in need of a more powerful machine. I had made lots of discoveries as I took more online courses, bought books and magazines and did my own experiments. I was still enjoying the third-age discussion group where we shared our ideas of graphics and photography, displaying our images on web pages. I started playing with the flat-bed scanner and came up with a series where I filled Japanese miniature vases with fresh flowers that I placed on the glass of the scanner. I imported the image into Photoshop then printed it out. Egged-on by Ken and my enthusiastic third-age online friends, I did more experiments. The trouble was that I was making very large files and the scanning could take up to twenty minutes for just one picture. I bought a more powerful computer and a more powerful flat-bed scanner. Then I really took off and had a lot of fun.

On September 11, 2001, with the awful news of the terrorist destruction of the World Trade Center, David postponed his intended trip from LA to London. He and Ken had a long conversation of how war and aggression affects people's lives enormously. As

From the flat bed scanner. Miniature Japanese vase with clematis and honeysuckle. An early scannergraph 2001.

Ken said: 'They certainly affected mine in 1944 when at the age of eighteen I was taken from being an apprentice scenic artist to be a coalminer — without so much as a by-your-leave. It was all a long time ago but my life changed very much because of it.' He had vivid memories: 'Wakened by alarm clock at 4 am on cold rainy winters morning to go to a Hell on earth in the bowels of that earth. Hot dusty dark, three-quarters-of-a-mile underground. Very dangerous working in tunnels no higher than a table leg. I remember it quite well — no medals or awards for the Bevin boys. You didn't look for the enemy it was all around you. Pit props snapping bringing tons of earth down, noxious gases, in many cases explosions. I remember it far too well.'

David spent a few nights with us ready for his film and the book-launch of *Secret Knowledge* on October 13, 2001. Ken was painting still-lifes extremely well; but he was worried and full of self-doubt. He said: 'As in the past when things are going well with painting I lose interest. It is almost as though I was afraid to paint a good picture in case it became successful. Why? I don't really know.'

Ken's hernia was dragging him down yet again and his wound was still not healing. He had another appointment with the hernia doctor who diagnosed infected mesh and operated under local anaesthetic. He assured Ken that it was not cancer. A few days later Ken got a message that his GP wanted to see him. It was bonfire day November 5, 2001, and Ken said that he got 'a right cracker today'. The doctor confirmed Ken's worst fear that he did have cancer. He had secondary cancer of the prostate but the primary source was not known. The doctor said that marvellous strides had been made in the treatment of this curse.

Ken got an appointment with the urinary surgeon for tests and possible surgery. On the due day he reported:

now developing sneezy wheezy. Just the job for anaesthesia — what a bloody peculiar hand I am getting in this game. Talk about come in number five your time's up, thank God I can be cynical about it.

I have booked a 'smoking' room at Belvedere hospital. I get the feeling that whatever I do is immaterial now — smoking dancing or singing arias makes no damned difference. The hearse has gone why bother to shut the gate.

He had the tests: liver, lymph and spleen OK, but kidneys not functioning properly and thickening of the aorta. Apart from that, 'hunky dory', but he had to go for a bone-scan the following week.

He wrote in his diary:

I must not become obsessed by my kidney function now. I wish 'they' did not tell me these things. My fertile imagination picks them up and makes a great drama out of them. Put Edgar Allan Poe in the back yard. I am losing my independence and I don't like it at all. Now taking hormone tablets.

Edgar Allan Poe said: 'I became insane, with long intervals of horrible sanity.'

David phoned sympathising with Ken, talking mostly about family and the value of love. Sic transit Gloria Mundi: all the glories of the world are soon passing, was their goodbye phrase. Thank God for humour because that kept us going. The bone-scan showed some old rib injury. Kidney function was getting slowly better. Prostate trouble was much-reduced, the groin-swelling less. In short the hormone was kicking in. No more appointments were needed for two months.

Ken got renewed vigour and painted most days. Whilst in Malibu he had made a watercolour painting of David's house. He was now copying that onto three canvases to make a triptych in acrylic paint. It was a joyous, colourful painting evoking happy memories. He also enjoyed painting still life and when David visited he admired them and encouraged Ken to keep painting.

We did talk about Ken dying and me living alone in such a large house. You can't plan these things but we briefly wondered about

Ken's painting of Malibu. David wrote the message to Paul and sent it via fax, so Paul would receive it as a black and white picture.

moving to a smaller house. Dream on. We decided that moving would intrude too much on whatever time was left to enjoy. Ken decided that 'Life after death is whatever you want it to be'. That idea made the thought of dying a bit more comforting. He got a clean bill of health for another year, so we made the most of it. Life was good. We had trips all over East and North Yorkshire. Ken would sketch or paint. I took photographs.

David came up from London. He was painting in water-colour, both landscapes and portraits. He went to Norway and did a lot of water-colour painting there, making use of the wonderful light. He visited us quite often in Bridlington and would always paint new portraits of us. Some of them show the stresses we were inevitably going through but Ken was always happy to sit and be painted.

Gradually Ken declined as pain extended throughout his body. He told his diary:

Aches pains hot flushes stiff muscles — treating them as rheumatics. Taking solpadeine and anadin galore. Totally obsessed with bowels — what a state to come to. I went a walk on the cliff with effort. Neck and back of head are very painful on movement. This diary is getting more like a medical report by the day. I must stop writing every little detail.

He had treatment with radiotherapy to zap the hot spots of his pain, which were mainly along his spine.

Ken also had some intravenous panidronate treatment at the Hospice, and became friendly with Simon, the male nurse in charge of the treatment. Simon and his wife Philippa and family visited us to see Ken's paintings. Simon was also very interested in my computer set-up. He became a lifeline if I needed help with the computer and when I wanted a yet more powerful machine he made it and set it all up for me. Ken and I had a friend, Tony Hogan, who opened an art gallery at Rudston a few miles away. He had always loved Ken's paintings and in September, 2002, started selling for him. This was great for Ken because he was not good at selling his own pictures, he would often give them away. Tony was impressed with my Japanese vase series of scans and I got them mounted and framed. To my delight they started selling too. What a shame that our joint-success would be so short-lived.

By October, 2002, David had painted twenty double portraits in water-colour and was keen to do one of Ken and me. We thought

Double portrait painting in water colour 2002.

maybe he would change his mind when he saw how we had aged with Ken's illness. David came with some new water-colour brush pens that he gave Ken to use along with a sketchbook. He did a very quick sketch of Ken with the new pens and planned next day to do our portraits in the studio. Ken was worried because he had pain in the chest, was hoarse, anxious and had hot flushes. It turned out to be a lovely day's experience, which did us both good.

That was August 19, 2002. Next day David did another drawing of us in the kitchen.

John came over from Australia and stayed a few weeks. He went off on tours to visit old friends and places. He was now a member of the Australian Story Telling Guild and was really happy with his new life. He visited schools, seniors and care-homes. He was particularly excited about the success he was having, evoking memories for patients with dementia.

I had a massive collection of books relating to alternative health studies and some diagnostic equipment that I no longer needed. I subscribed to eBay and Amazon and had frequent sales. David asked whether I could locate three volumes of Rembrandt drawings. I did a world search on Abe books and found them in Canada. They cost over £500 but David was happy with that price so I arranged to have them delivered to him. Another amazing discovery of what the Internet made possible.

Ken and I continued with our country drives, sketching and photography. He had morphia patches, oramorph and hormones and needed lots of help with daily living. A problem for me was communication at night. Without the hearing aids I could hear nothing whatsoever and I couldn't sleep in them as they would whistle. I rigged up a system of flex extensions that plugged into a bright bedside lamp so that Ken could press a switch by his bed and it would shine a light onto my face to wake me up. A few years later I had a hearing dog, vibrating iPhone, wireless doorbells and lots more options, but at the time my set-up worked all right. I fixed another lamp downstairs in the kitchen, using the same method. Ken would spend most of the morning in bed and

Making the most of what time he had left: Ken painting in studio a few months before he died.

Margaret   and   Ken
16th June 03.   love

Here we are again, for the last time, painted by David a few days before Ken was admitted to the hospice in June 2003.

we would go out in the afternoons. A favourite trip was to Tony's art gallery and Ken was especially happy when Tony had a class of students with whom he could discuss their paintings. As well as the drives Ken continued to paint most days even if he had to keep his dressing-gown on. I set up a table so he could sit down and paint in water-colour when standing at the easel became too painful.

David visited again to paint water-colour portraits. Ken on June 15, 2003, and mine on June 16. These would be the last before Ken died.

I was becoming more proficient with Photoshop and I worked on the image to make it more 'arty' mainly by using layers and blending the layers. I scanned irises, nasturtiums, roses and poppies and as the flowers appeared in the garden they would head for the scanner. The first dozen were a great success. I was happy with them and Ken was delighted. I called them the Summer Collection. Tony wanted to sell them in the gallery as soon as they were framed. I had an A3 printer, which would be active for hours at a time printing out an edition of each: a marvellous hobby and, being creative, I could enjoy the mornings and be refreshed when Ken was ready for help.

Suddenly on June 20, 2003, Ken could not bear weight on his leg. We struggled on for a few days, but my help was not enough and he was in great discomfort. His hip X-ray showed a patho-

Poppy profile from the Summer collection of scannergraphs.

logical fracture. To my surprise he was admitted to hospital for a hip-replacement. Seemingly this was the only way that the pain could be relieved. He could never bear weight again so had to be admitted to a very caring hospice where I spent many hours with him. I carried on framing my Summer Collection but when they were ready, I was reluctant to celebrate.

Tony wanted to have a preview at the gallery. Ken was very ill but he asked me whether I had put them on show yet. He insisted that I took them to the gallery and had the preview. I sold five on the opening night and excitedly told Ken. He gave the thumbs-up sign. Next day he died. I was with him as he breathed his last on July 28, 2003.

Sophie and Charlie were our miniature dachshunds, both-ten-years old. When Ken was admitted to the hospice his beloved Sophie missed him dreadfully. I would sometimes take the dogs to visit him, never quite sure whether doing so helped or hindered any of them. Short-haired Sophie lost her appetite and started getting bald patches that became red and messy. I got cream from the vet but it didn't help much. I also gave her Bach flower remedies for her stress. From the day Ken died she got worse and wanted to remain in her bed under a blanket. I would carry her to the garden where she obliged with toileting but she wanted no food and scarcely any water.

Within a week she could no longer walk, her body was covered in sores and she showed no interest whatsoever in Charlie, me, or life in general. The vet and I agreed that she had no will to live without her lifelong companion Ken. It was another sad day as I held her close and told her to find Ken. The vet euthanised her into a final sleep. A few months after Ken's funeral, their ashes were scattered together into the sea.

Sophie, Ken's beloved dog, pined away and died soon after he did.

21 Bigger Technology

For the first couple of days after the funeral David stayed with me. We drove along country roads towards Goathland on the North Yorkshire moors where the heather was luscious and sheep were grazing. Next day we went to the beautiful pastures of Millington in East Yorkshire, so green, peaceful and perfect. We took picnics to avoid shops and crowds. Then I went to stay with Pauline for a few days in Harrogate. Philip and Mary visited from Australia. Life drifted along,

In January 2004, David came to stay again. He knew for sure that he wanted to paint Yorkshire. He made a few water-colour paintings of Woldgate. They were bold colours; I think there was gouache in them as well. He was also forever painting in his sketchbooks. He kept leaving for London, America, Norway or Spain then coming back to paint in Bridlington. His comings-and-goings made life very exciting. He never came alone so there would be quite a crowd including his own cook and helpers, leaving me free to continue my scanning and learning on the computer. David was pleased to see that I was busy. He wondered about including some 'hand-work' in my scans before I printed them. I had to point out that I was the only one in the family who could not draw, so that was not an option. Anyway I was doing all right, slowly selling my creations.

We got talking about Photoshop. He had used it when it was a rather slow process. I showed him how it had vastly-improved. We scanned one of his sketchbooks and he Photo-shopped out the dark centre-line where I merged the two sides of the sketchbook. Before long he was painting portraits with a Wacom pad and pen directly into Photoshop on the computer. I also pointed out to David that he could email his pictures to the studio in Los Angeles, in fact anywhere in the world. We had to make sure that the image was optimised so it could be viewed clearly on the screen but would not have enough resolution for printing. If he wanted them printed in Los Angeles then it was also possible to send full resolution images. He painted a series of twenty-one Yorkshire landscapes in water-colour. I either took photos or scanned those paintings and printed them. They were printed on Super A3 heavyweight matte paper (thirteen by nineteen inches). In twenty-four hours I used twelve ink cartridges. Normally I might go through four cartridges a day printing my scans, but this was a bit mad.

Me and my big brother 2005.

Life was hectic with computing, visitors, trips out and good meals. Then all of a sudden David and his entourage would be gone. I needed a couple of days to catch up with washing, tidying and just being alone again. Other visitors came. Philip and Mary brought two of their grand-daughters, Sarah and Rachel.

I was still selling scans at Tony Hogan's gallery and a whole group of us became friendly: Tony and Eileen, Rob, Liz and Jonathan, Merice and Glen. Five of us went on holiday to Venice and had a marvellous time. Three were painting, two of us took photographs. Tony arranged a Venice exhibition of our creative endeavours that was very successful. Simon, who nursed Ken at the Hospice, was a regular visitor when I needed help with computer problems.

I was feeling the strain of not hearing people and at times felt dizzy again. Blood pressure was up and down along with the tempo of my life. Jean Pierre, one of David's assistants, also known as JP, was very bright and keen to help with the photographing of pictures. He is a musician, plays an accordion and said that he had not taken up photography before. I lent him one of my cameras, the Olympus 740, and within a month he had taken over five thousand excellent photos, many of them of David painting, with the focus on the end of the paintbrush. He wanted to learn how to use Photoshop. At that time I was using Windows computers and David's people each had a Mac laptop. So I had to try and get used to the Mac in order to set JP on track to learning. He was quick and organised his photographs most competently. At the end of a day out painting, JP would show us the whole sequence of photos, viewed as a slide show with very short intervals. It was another exciting way to use the computer and digital camera.

As David observed my scanning and digital photography the idea dawned on him that there was a whole new way of making large multi-canvas oil paintings. He would make a sketch or paint an intended subject, then take a photo and print it out and make a grid of the number of canvases he wanted to use. From the grid he could plan each canvas and paint one at a time, then photograph each one at a size that would fit on the studio wall and in his bedroom. He always liked to review current pictures from his bed. When David has a good idea it tends to escalate quickly. JP and his helpers made painting on location possible by transporting a whole set of canvases and reinforced easels in a shelved Toyota van.

What always amazed me about David was how he saw the way he did. He painted *Woldgate Woods* in all four seasons of the year. I had been driving up and down Woldgate for years but could not identify where he painted those pictures. He gave me the exact location and it turned out to be a spot where I had often walked with the dogs. There was usually a bit of fly-tipped junk around there. I finally saw what he had seen and it was quite beautiful. A half-turn of the head would be in sight of an ugly old TV set and maybe a fridge or mattress. I remembered: 'We see things not as they are but as we are'. He looked at the sheer beauty of the place, I had only noticed the rubbish. He worked with the seasons; May to June was particularly busy because that is when the beautiful hawthorn blooms. Seeing the trees laden with white blossom was always uplifting; but David made it even more special by emphasising the sheer abundance and beauty of that annual event.

Little Charlie, the long-haired dachshund, died in August, almost a year after Sophie. The house was full and Charlie had visited everyone in their separate rooms, seemingly to say goodbye. He had been breathless for a couple of days and he came to sit beside me at the computer. I told him to stay put whilst I brought him fresh water from the kitchen. When I returned he had died. He was such a dear little fellow. When David and the gang left next day I missed him very much and felt really alone. No barking when the doorbell rang meant that I had to be more alert than ever, listening for visitors and parcel deliveries. In November, 2004, I got a text phone. It was a great help because all my art friends had them and if they visited they could text when they arrived at the door. I could feel the vibration in my pocket and that little phone became a lifeline.

Early in 2005, Liz and Eileen asked me if I would submit three scans to the Royal Academy Summer Exhibition. They were sending some of their own entries. I thought they were joking, didn't think any of us had any hope whatsoever. I wasn't even sure that my scans counted as art. They offered to take mine to London and had a submission form for me so I said, maybe. Later, as I was shopping in the supermarket, my eyes were scanning the fruit and vegetables for ideas. Then I noticed the fresh-fish counter. I bought an octopus and a dozen sprats and by the following evening I had printed out three scans on super A3 sized Epson watercolour paper: one of the octopus, one enlarged sprat, and for the third one I overlaid the sprat onto the octopus and called it sprat-opus. They were duly framed, submitted and forgotten about. I got a letter scarcely a week before the Summer Exhibition 2005 opened in June telling me that the *Scanned Octopus* had been accepted and hung. The other two works were passed through the first round and awarded 'doubtful' status but were not hung. Even though I thought it was beginner's luck it was a massive confidence boost. Ken would have been delighted: he loved the ambience of the Royal

Academy of Arts and had been a friend and visitor for many years. I went with him to the Summer Exhibition every year.

Two weeks later on my seventieth birthday, I had a wonderful day. David invited me to Royal Ascot at York. Normally Royal Ascot is held in Windsor; but while the racecourse was being renovated they moved to York for the year. We were in the Royal enclosure with the Duke and Duchess of Devonshire on the last day of a five-day event. The sun shone brightly. I even won £700 on the horses, enough to buy a new camera.

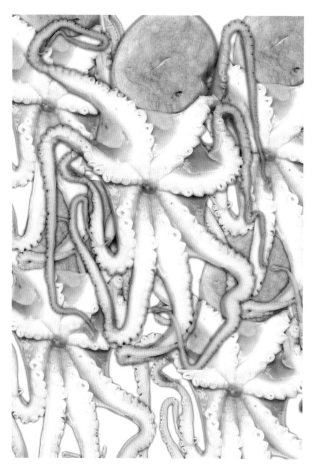

This scanned octopus was hung in the Royal Academy Summer Exhibition.

If only I had been twenty years younger or not had hearing problems maybe I could perhaps have joined the group assisting David with computing and photography. Working among a great team of people would have been a wonderful life. David would be up as the sun rose and be out painting most of the day. There was always something interesting happening and new paintings to see. Trouble was that even though life was good, whether I was alone or surrounded by people, I was finding intensity too unstable for my health. Life was either a feast or a famine. I was dizzy and unbalanced again and could hardly keep up with the race of life and everything I wanted to do. I was still sorting out things of Ken's and had suitcases full of Mum's diaries and letters that I was hoping to read.

Doctor prescribed tablets to stabilise the fluctuating blood pressure, but I reacted very badly to them. I got an awful cough and became breathless with the least exertion, so could no longer enjoy my daily beach walks. Then, to make matters worse, I got pains in my feet so that even walking round the house became painful. I knew that I needed to make some life-changes. In December 2005, I moved out of Kingston Road to a dormer bungalow five minutes walk away.

David soon filled the house with people, computers and equipment. He employed Jonathan Wilkinson as technical and computer assistant. He continued painting Yorkshire and rented a large warehouse to make an absolutely enormous studio with wall space for all his bigger pictures. I visited regularly to keep up-to-date. He was to have a massive exhibition in the Royal Academy in 2012, all twelve rooms filled with his work. Naturally, he became very busy preparing for that event.

I kept trying different blood pressure tablets, but finally abandoned them because of all the side effects. I had three bedrooms and three outbuildings so there was plenty of space for storing and sorting. One of the bedrooms became a sewing room, and a downstairs room became a computer room. Gradually with my own herbs and more stable lifestyle my health improved. On the Internet I discovered some rocker-soled shoes that I could buy in York. They instantly relieved the pain in my feet. I have worn that type of shoe ever since, initially MBT's but also Chung Shi and Skechers shape-ups.

I carried on with my scanning. Liz, one of the artist friends, opened her own gallery in Bridlington Old Town and I had two exhibitions there. The first was a series called *Larger than Life* and the next was called *Fluid Scans*. I blew bubbles on the scanner, broke eggs and poured paint on the glass. It was fun, experimenting and keeping fluid on the surface without letting it leak through into the scanner itself.

In September 2009, I was partnered with a two-year-old lowchen hearing dog called Sally. She was trained to tap me if the doorbell rang and alert me to fire and smoke alarms as well as the kitchen timer. I took her everywhere. Wearing her maroon hearing dog coat and lead she was allowed in shops, restaurants and had other privileges along with

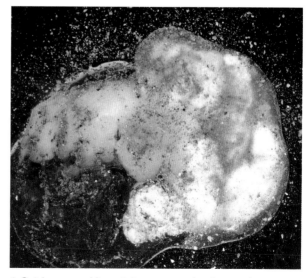

A fluid scanned by mixing egg and paint on the scanner.

Sally, my faithful Hearing Dog.

those for guide dogs for the blind. She became my devoted companion, always alert on my behalf.

About the same time, Philip and Mary visited from Australia. We went out for a family meal with David, Paul and Jean. Philip showed us his iPhone and our lives changed forever. David and Paul each got one within a week of Philip leaving. I swapped my little text phone for an iPhone 4. Paul, David and I would compare the latest app or function on these amazing devices. In my search for graphic and kaleidoscope apps I came across Brushes. I showed it to David but at first he didn't seem too interested. He was busy shaving with an iPhone razor and playing the mouth organ on it. Very soon however the Brushes app was in use and by April, 2009, David was emailing vases of fresh flowers or sunrises painted with the Brushes app nearly every morning. David had overtaken me with his use of digital technology.

I was most intrigued when I first saw a Jeep driving slowly up and down Woldgate with nine top-of-the-range high-definition digital cameras mounted in a weird contraption on the bonnet. David was inside where he could see the viewfinders and set each camera at

slightly different angles: such a strange and rather amusing sight to
encounter on that quiet country lane in East Yorkshire. They all looked
so busy and serious. JP and Jonathan Wilkinson were on the outside,
sometimes up a ladder, taking instructions how to adjust the cameras.
I had no idea what they were doing.

All was revealed when I visited the studio in Kingston Road. There
was a wall of eighteen monitors. Nine monitors for each side of the
road. Each monitor was playing back videos from separate cameras.
The edges of each were perfectly aligned with the next one. He repeated
this in *Spring, Summer, Autumn and Winter*. What a fantastic series it
was.

Meanwhile I upgraded my iPhone so I could experiment with pano-
ramas, time-lapse, slo-mo and generally have fun taking my simple
photos. And I carried on scanning. I was finding my equipment bag
of cameras and lenses too heavy to carry, so I gradually made the
iPhone my primary camera. It was always in my pocket. Paul was also
sending Brushes pictures from his iPhone. They were very good and
he and I shared an exhibition of our work at Liz's gallery. In 2010, the
iPad was released and David was soon sending email pictures from his
iPad. Incredibly his Brushes paintings were making enormous-sized
prints, which would be hung on the wall of the warehouse studio. He
spent a lot more time along Woldgate painting *The Arrival of Spring*
on his iPad. When David had his Bigger Exhibition at the Royal
Academy in 2012 all the family came over from Australia, and we got
together for a celebratory dinner at Langhan's brasserie.

Two years later Paul and his wife Jean left Flamborough and were
living nearer to their family in Baildon. They were planning another
move into a retirement complex. David was painting portraits in Los
Angeles. Within a couple of years I would be eighty and was asking
myself whether I was in the best place for the rest of my life. I didn't
feel particularly old and was still busy every day: sewing, computing,
driving and walking the dog and of course meeting my art friends.

I remembered reading an article in *The Guardian*, an interview with
Diana Athill: 'Why I Moved into an Old People's Home'. I checked it
out on the Internet and re-read it. She said: 'I had not realised that an
old person can be reduced to helplessness almost overnight'. I lived
alone, couldn't hear a telephone and had no desire to be reduced to
helplessness; nor did I want anyone to feel the need to care for me. I
decided to look at options. My favourite choice was to buy a property

A bit of a do at Langhan's brasserie, London, 2012. Back: David, Middle: Philip, me, Paul, Front: John. Photo by Ian HIll.

in a purpose-built retirement village, so I could remain independent but live in a safe environment with help and meals available if or when I needed them. So that is what I did. Down-sizing is not easy. I sold books on Amazon and miscellaneous items galore on eBay. I made lots of donations to charity and sold a few large items in the local auction rooms. Then in October, 2014, I moved from East to North Yorkshire and am now very comfortable. I have had time to read the diaries that Mum wrote, the archived material of my father and the diaries that Ken wrote. I have read all my letters that Mum saved along with lots of memorabilia of my own that I had saved.

We all have a story of our lives. This is my story so far.